Bloody Good Shakespeare

How Pop-up Globe made audiences
fall back in love with the Bard

Miles Gregory

HENSLOWE
IRVING
PRESS

First Edition: Henslowe Irving Press, April 2025
Set in Garamond.

O For a Muse of Fire, that would ascend
The brightest Heaven of Invention:
A Kingdom for a Stage, Princes to Act,
And Monarchs to behold the swelling Scene.
Henry V

This book is dedicated to the Pop-up Globe Theatre Company 2015 – 2020, our audiences, my parents Jim and Trish, and my family – my inspirational wife and co-collaborator Bob, and our children Nancy, Adelaide, Rupert and Florence.

Contents

Introduction

TEN YEARS AGO, IN April 2015, I announced plans to build the world's first full-scale, temporary, working replica of Shakespeare's second Globe theatre. Ten months later, in February 2016, Pop-up Globe opened in Auckland, New Zealand.

What followed exceeded all expectations. For four extraordinary years, the company brought Shakespeare to hundreds of thousands of people. Then, in an echo of Shakespeare's own world, plague closed the playhouses.

I created Pop-up Globe to test a belief: that Shakespeare, performed in a certain way, in a certain space, can create an absolutely remarkable and unforgettable experience. Pop-up Globe affirmed this belief, and exceeded it, time and time again.

I never set out to write a book about directing Shakespeare. But after nearly three decades of studying, teaching, directing and producing his work, and having had the frankly outrageous fortune of building more Globe theatres than Shakespeare himself, it felt time to set down what I'd learned. What I'd tried. What worked. And what emphatically didn't.

This is a handbook, not a memoir. Though informed by my experience – especially as founding artistic director of Pop-up Globe – it is not *about* that story. Nor is it a scholarly treatise, though I hope scholars find it sufficiently rigorous. Its aim is simple: to offer anyone directing, acting, or teaching Shakespeare a practical method for making productions that audiences love. One that honours the spirit of the plays while making them vivid and clear for today's audiences.

Why now? Because what happened at Pop-up Globe was special. The spirit that animated our productions deserves to be recorded, however imperfectly. And to the best of my knowledge, it's the first time a New Zealander has dared to write a book about how to direct Shakespeare. We have archives, production histories, scholarly essays, prompt books, and memoirs. But not a single practical guide. Nothing that says: here's one way to do it.

The same is mostly true in Australia. For generations, Australian actors toured the Bard from goldfields to capital cities. But it wasn't until John Bell's memoir *On Shakespeare* in 2011 that an Australasian actor-director's approach made it into print. Bell's book is wise, generous, and reflective – but it's not, and doesn't claim to be, a method.

This book *is*.

That may sound grand. It isn't meant to. Naturally I don't claim this method is the *only* way to direct Shakespeare. But it is *a* way – a way that I've forged in rehearsal rooms around the world, over hundreds of performances, in a wide variety of conditions and with all kinds of people. Professionals. Students. Amateurs. It's a method that works, especially for audiences – and even actors – who think they don't like Shakespeare. It's flexible, practical, and designed to liberate the text in performance.

A word about Pop-up Globe. From 2015 to 2020, the theatre I founded brought some 750,000 people to Shakespeare in New Zealand and Australia. We built five full-scale replica Globes – two in Auckland, and one each in Perth, Melbourne, and Sydney – and filled them with joyful performances. We staged eighteen full-scale Shakespeare productions, most in repertory, and employed hundreds of artists. At our peak, we produced more Shakespeare than any other company in the Southern Hemisphere.

I wanted to make this project in New Zealand because I felt I owed something to this place. I am a fifth-generation Kiwi on my mother's side. After leaving New Zealand at the age of seventeen and spending the next seventeen years in the United Kingdom, I came back with a deep sense of debt to the country I was born in, raised in, and shaped by. Growing up in New Zealand taught me lifelong lessons about leadership, courage, determination, and sacrifice. Creating Pop-up Globe here was, in part, an act of gratitude.

I also knew that the Kiwi spirit of ingenuity – of finding innovative ways around seemingly insurmountable obstacles – would find a fitting challenge in creating a full-scale working Globe replica out of steel, wood, and paint.

In some ways, Pop-up Globe was a uniquely Kiwi approach to Shakespeare. As the great Kiwi physicist Ernest Rutherford almost put it, we didn't have the money, so we had to think. And many of the productions we made were uniquely Kiwi too – born directly or indirectly born out of the complex partnership between Māori and Pākehā, mediated through the flexible and ever-adaptive spirit of Shakespeare, here in the South Seas.

In this sense, just as Aotearoa New Zealand has long been a place where cultures intermingle and generate new ways of expressing the human condition, so too did Shakespeare's plays function on the Pop-up Globe stage. For this reason, I focus mostly on the way we made Shakespeare at Pop-up Globe in those short four years – because this Shakespeare was my hard experience put into practice. That practice, in turn, led to even more hard-won lessons – lessons now distilled in this book.

But this book is not a victory lap. Nor is it a monument. In truth, Pop-up Globe nearly broke me. The highs were matched by intense personal, professional, and spiritual pressure. That story will be told elsewhere, if at all. This book is not about the journey. It's about the gold that we found while we were on it.

If you're a first-time director, I hope this book gives you confidence. If you're an actor, I hope it sharpens your choices. If you're a teacher, I hope it helps bring Shakespeare alive in your classroom. And if you're an experienced theatre-maker, I hope it sparks dialogue and inspiration.

Onwards.

Bloody Good Shakespeare

The playhouse was packed. A hot Auckland night, the air humming with energy. The standing yard thronged, the galleries buzzing. Expectation crackled. Opening night of my production of *Twelfth Night*, Pop-up Globe, 2016. And as Pop-up Globe's founder and artistic director, I was in the thick of it – but tonight, playing the role of an usher. The front of house team needed the help, and I needed to be in the crowd, to feel what they felt.

A young woman approached, her partner in tow. She was excited. He was not. Still in his hi-vis, straight from the site, he had the look of a man who wanted to be anywhere else.

I showed them to their seats and forgot about them. The show began. The audience was with us from the first moment. They gasped, laughed, cheered. They became part of the story. And when it ended – after the final dance, after the actors had left the stage, when the applause finally died – they didn't rush for the exits. They lingered, buzzing.

Then I saw them again. The couple. But this time, the husband was leading. He strode towards me, emotion on his face, his wife plucking at his arm. I braced myself.

He stopped, jabbed a finger at me, searching for words.

That was...

A pause. A shake of his head.

I wasn't expecting it, he said. *But it was bloody good.*

And that was it. He turned and walked off. His wife smiled, and followed him.

But in that moment, I knew we were on to something special. We had taken a man who had no reason to care about Shakespeare, and connected with him. We had upended his expectations. Given him a night he'd remember forever. Taken 'high art' and made it accessible. Turned a Kiwi tradie into a Shakespeare fan.

That is the highest praise: not from a critic, not from a scholar, but from someone who came expecting boredom, but left electrified.

That reaction – the surprise, the joy, the sheer aliveness of it – is how Shakespeare must have affected audiences four hundred years ago, and how it should affect them still today. It's what we built Pop-up Globe to do. This is the effect produced by making *Bloody Good Shakespeare*.

Why this book exists

This is why I've written this book. To share some of the knowledge I've learned by hard experience in the hope that more young people – and even hardened professionals – are inspired by participating in the power of performed Shakespeare.

After three decades immersed in Shakespeare's world, working with thousands of actors, directing countless productions, I've gathered insights that can't be found in academic texts alone. These lessons came through trial and error, through successes and failures on stages across multiple continents.

This experience has revealed practical wisdom about what makes Shakespeare accessible, exciting, and transformative for modern audiences – from technical aspects of staging and performance to deeper understandings of how these centuries-old works can create profound connections with us in the here-and-now.

This book distills what I've discovered through passionate and sometimes painful exploration with professional theatremakers and demanding audiences.

I'm not presenting these ideas as definitive answers – Shakespeare's work is too rich and multifaceted for any single approach. Rather, I'm offering them as tested pathways that might help others who share this passion, whether they're directors, actors, educators, or simply people who believe in the enduring power of these plays.

The techniques and philosophies shared in these pages emerged from real-world application, from watching audiences respond, from listening to actors discover new dimensions in familiar texts, and from constantly questioning my own assumptions about how Shakespeare connects with us today.

My hope is that by sharing these hard-won lessons, I might contribute something meaningful to our collective understanding of how to keep Shakespeare's extraordinary body of work alive and deeply relevant for generations to come.

Why is it so important that we keep performing and watching Shakespeare? It would be easy to let him go. He is dead. Long dead. A provincial player turned royal favourite, writing in an age that tortured animals for sport and burned dissenters at the stake. His world was bloodier, bawdier, and Godly in a way ours barely remembers.

Why persist, then? Why press these old words, these tangled plots, these ghosts and fools and kings into the hands of each new generation?

The simplest answer is because Shakespeare's plays still work.

He summons the raw materials of the human condition: love and ambition, fear and faith, despair and joy. He is not tame. He does not coddle. He tells the truth in heightened music, and his truth is still truth. Somehow, in the words of this long dead man from Stratford, we still see ourselves reflected.

For any English speaker, Shakespeare is our foundational text. His plays are cathedrals of language built on the bedrock of being human. Shakespeare shows what people are, what power does, what guilt costs. He dramatizes prayer, madness, forgiveness, revenge – in action, in speech, in bodies.

His plays are whole worlds, and observing them brings us insight and meaning. In this sense, he helps us understand ourselves. Watching Shakespeare is a sort of ancient therapy.

But he also brings us together. A theatre is a kind of chapel. A performance of Shakespeare brings together people who do not know each other and binds them in shared wonder.

In his best moments, he creates communion. He offers a ritual that renews our speech, our empathy, and our ability to listen. The act of gathering for Shakespeare is itself an act of resistance to the algorithms that divide us, to the fragmentation of modern life.

Yes, he requires some effort. He asks us to hear through unfamiliar syntax and feel beyond easy meaning. In doing so, he stretches the muscle of imagination, both for actor and audience. In a time when so much is shallow, screen-fed, and short-form, Shakespeare deepens and lengthens attention. He strengthens the root system of our human culture.

We continue to perform Shakespeare as a declaration of what matters. His theatre is a forge where the human spirit is tested, tempered, and revealed. And in the age that is upon us – divided, fragmented, increasingly filled with fluent simulations of humanity – we will need his clarity more than ever.

Shakespeare shows us what Artificial Intelligence cannot: the weight of conscience, the ache of mercy, the glory and grief of being fully alive. In short, he teaches us how to be human. That's why we've got to keep performing him in ways that bring him fully to life.

Why this book now?

In a world saturated with algorithm-driven entertainment, why should anyone still bother with live theatre? Why would Shakespeare, a playwright dead for four centuries, still matter in the near future when audiences summon Artificial Intelligence-generated stories on demand?

I've glimpsed the future of entertainment up close. After plague closed the theatres in 2020, I co-founded an AI entertainment startup, working at the bleeding edge of personalised, automated, digital storytelling.

What I witnessed was revolutionary: the boundaries between film, television, and social media dissolving into a single stream of personalised digital content.

Soon, AI will transform these experiences into interactive, algorithm-driven narratives tailored to individual preferences, generating actors, dialogue, and visuals in real-time. Every screen will become a portal to entertainment that knows what you want before you do, and potentially knows you better than you know yourself.

Yet as digital experiences become more frictionless and perfect, what we'll need – what we'll crave – is their opposite: imperfection, unpredictability, presence, shared experience. Here is the theatre's renewed purpose. Not as competition to digital media, but as its essential counterbalance.

Theatre is the antidote to an algorithmic world. Shakespeare, performed with total commitment, taps into the deep shared centre of humanity, beyond our diverse surfaces. His work in performance becomes the perfect counterpoint to digital content because it is unrepeatable, immediate, human.

A screen will never look back at you and wink. An actor will. In that moment of eye contact, a connection is forged that is raw, electric, undeniable, ancient. When an audience listens together, laughs together, holds its collective breath, they become part of something larger than themselves.

No machine can echo the raw power of bodies gathered in space, of stories born and breathed in real time. Nothing rivals the electric shock we feel when our eyes meet those of another human. It is in this shockingly powerful connection that we feel most alive. And Shakespeare is a master of this connection.

Who is this book for?

This book is not an academic treatise. It is part manifesto, part practical guide. A demand that we stop treating Shakespeare as if he were delicate, untouchable, remote or worse, boring. His plays were written for the stage, for the people, for a theatre that pulsed with life. *Bloody Good Shakespeare* reclaims that spirit.

This book is for the directors seeking new ways to stage old texts. For producers who want Shakespeare that sells out theatres. For actors struggling with words buried under outdated tradition. For teachers desperate to make students feel Shakespeare rather than merely understand him. And for audiences – those burned by bad productions and those yet to be convinced that Shakespeare can be the most thrilling experience they'll ever have in a theatre.

Seven stops on my road to Pop-up Globe

Cheltenham Beach, New Zealand, 1985. I am eight years old, sitting in the front seat of my father's car, parked by Cheltenham Beach. The salt air seeps through the open window. My father, who loves the English language, recites from memory: *'Tis not so deep as a well, nor so wide as a church door, but 'tis enough, 'twill serve: ask for me tomorrow, and you shall find me a grave man.* He is smiling. I don't know the play. I don't even know who Mercutio is. But something about these playful, defiant, ancient words lodges in my mind. Who is this Shakespeare, who makes people joke as they die? The words feel like a message from another time, and I want to understand them.

Auckland, New Zealand, 1991. Fourteen years old. My friends and I, armed with broom handles, are rehearsing a scene from *Romeo and Juliet* in an empty classroom. I've edited it down, stripped it to its essentials, made it faster, sharper. *This shall determine that!* I shout, lunging forward. We have no audience, no costumes, no proper swords. But to my teenage self, *Romeo and Juliet* is raw, immediate, like a documentary of my own world. Saying these ancient words feels like making magic.

Durham, UK, April 1997. My girlfriend, Sophie, is sophisticated and clever and, crucially, president of the College theatre company. She persuades me to audition. I have no intention of becoming a theatre director. I imagine a future in law or diplomacy. But when she casts me in a summer tour of *The Tempest*, performing in grand English homes, something shifts. We are a company of friends, wearing hired Royal Shakespeare Company costumes, sleeping in tents on croquet lawns, piling into country pubs after every show. It is life-changing. I don't want it to end.

Exeter, March 2000. I am sitting in the Jolly Porter pub with my colleague Dom. We are each supposed to be staging a single scene for our MFA in Staging Shakespeare. Instead, we form a whole new theatre company, British Touring Shakespeare. Within months, our company of twenty actors is performing full-scale productions of *Much Ado About Nothing* and *A Midsummer Night's Dream*, playing to audiences who find them hilarious while we feel we are only scratching the surface. We rehearse in fifteenth-century gatehouses, perform in front of impossibly beautiful castles. It is life on a higher plane.

London, January 2001. I stand in the foyer of the Westminster Theatre, meeting with my theatre company on the last day of our run. Our productions of *Hamlet* and *Twelfth Night* have drawn audiences and critical acclaim on tour in the Middle East, and here in our London run. At twenty-three, I am – for a while at least – the youngest director working in the West End. The stakes feel impossibly high. The pressure is relentless. There is no safety net. But I am learning something invaluable: theatre is risk, and the greater the risk, the greater the reward.

Bristol, August 2008. It has been four years since I founded the Bristol Shakespeare Festival. I am sprawling under a three-hundred year old oak in Queen Square with Ben, the festival's associate producer, watching a production set up around us. My PhD is finished. The festival has grown beyond anything I imagined. Ben asks me what's next. *I want to run a theatre*, I say. Six weeks later, I am invited to become artistic director and CEO of The Maltings in Berwick, England's northernmost theatre. I accept.

Auckland, June 2014. It's been two years since I left The Maltings in excellent hands, our audiences tripled, our funding quadrupled, my work complete. Now I'm on the other side of the world, sitting with my four-year-old daughter Nancy and her little sister Adelaide. I read them a pop-up storybook. A miniature of Shakespeare's original Globe Theatre unfolds before us. *Can we go there?* Nancy asks. *No, it's a long way away,* I start to say.

But then I stop. I think. A 'pop-up' Globe. Could such a thing be possible? It strikes me as the greatest challenge I've ever encountered. That night, I talk to my wife. We have $10,000 in savings. We decide to risk it all.

Nineteen months later, in February 2016, after an unforgettable adventure that is a story in itself, the first Pop-up Globe opens in a carpark in Auckland. We're just in time for the four-hundredth anniversary of Shakespeare's death. The response is remarkable.

Pop-up Globe's first Auckland season in 2016 attracts over 100,000 people in just twelve weeks, making it the largest theatre event in New Zealand history. Through a five-year journey, the company produces nineteen productions across four cities in two countries, delighting over 750,000 people through-out Australasia.

By embracing Shakespeare's original performance conditions – shared light, no amplification, direct address, fast-paced storytelling – while infusing them with theatrical spectacle, we connect with diverse audiences. People who had previously avoided Shakespeare return repeatedly, bringing their friends and family. Our Melbourne season alone draws 146,000 people in a five month, twice-extended run. Pop-up Globe becomes more than a Shakespearean re-vival – it's a historic cultural phenomenon.

What makes it so special is not the playhouse, although this is the perfect setting for Shakespeare's work. It's the productions themselves. Shakespeare becomes a smash-hit again, four hundred years after his death.

The secret formula

What emerged in the Pop-up Globe adventure was a fundamental truth: made the right way, in the right spaces, Shakespeare remains as thrilling, popular, and relevant today as four centuries ago.

The secret formula of Pop-up Globe's popular success lay in making theatre that embraced the original spirit of Shakespeare's work while creating an atmosphere of genuine accessibility and excitement. We discovered that when performances balanced historical integrity with dynamic theatrical energy, when actors directly engaged the audience as active participants rather than passive observers, something magical happened.

Our productions combined meticulous attention to Shakespeare texts and Jacobean staging practices with a bold and expansive theatrical flair that spoke to contemporary audiences. By stripping away the reverence and academic distance that often surrounds Shakespeare, we revealed the raw, visceral pow-er of his storytelling. The blood, sweat, and laughter were real. The emotions were immediate.

What truly set Pop-up Globe apart was its unique ability to create commu-nity. Standing in the yard or seated in the galleries, audiences experienced Shakespeare as a shared, collective event rather than an isolated, intellectual exercise.

People from all walks of life – teenagers and grandparents, Shakespeare scholars and first-time theatregoers – found themselves responding together, collectively moved by the emotions flowing from the stage to the audience and back again.

This powerful group experience had an extraordinary impact on many audience members, particularly younger ones. Every evening the doors to the theatre would open and young people would rush in to get the closest spots to the stage, or to claim areas in the yard that they knew were close to the action.

As the phenomenon of seeing young people, teenagers, come back night after night, totally gripped by Shakespeare continued, I began to observe them more closely on my regular visits to the theatre. Clearly, they loved the risk of fluid spatter from the stage. They also delighted in being spoken to or noticed by the actors. But most of all, they seemed to be absolutely immersed in the emotion and spectacle of the story.

This was the most surprising thing – to see these young people, many of whom perhaps had previously seen Shakespeare as the most boring thing imaginable, transformed into 'emotion junkies' who returned on multiple occasions to the same production, standing as close to the stage as possible, even sometimes wearing home-made costumes in their favourite actor/character's honour. It was incredible to see how Shakespeare inspired these young people.

I've long believed that only good things can happen through exposure to Shakespeare. Engaging with Shakespeare builds confidence, proving to young people that they can grasp complex ideas, language, and emotions, opening the door to a lifetime of learning. For those who once believed Shakespeare was 'not for the likes of them', discovering an enjoyment of his work can be truly transformational, shattering barriers to culture and intellectual ambition. After all, if you can understand and enjoy Shakespeare, *there are surely no limits to what you can take on.*

Bloody Good Shakespeare

'Bloody good' is a solid Kiwi phrase. It means something outstanding, something undeniable.

But Bloody Good Shakespeare isn't just a turn of phrase. It's profoundly literal. Blood flows through Shakespeare's canon as both physical reality and potent metaphor, carrying life and signaling death in equal measure. Shakespeare connects blood to our deepest human paradox: the substance that sustains us also marks our mortality. Blood becomes the visual grammar through which Shakespeare encodes transgression, transformation, and the threshold between life and death. In a theatrical tradition where language reigns supreme, blood speaks a direct, universal truth that requires no translation.

Theatrical blood – that sticky, viscous fluid spilled across Pop-up Globe's boards – creates an physiological reaction in audiences. They know it's fake, yet it triggers something primal. Engaging with Bloody Good Shakespeare has a physical impact, heightening heart rate, stimulating brain activity, and triggering emotional and neurological responses.

Shakespeare's plays were never meant to be cultural vegetables, something consumed because they're 'good for you.' They were meant to be intoxicating feasts. When you stage Shakespeare this way – with blood that looks real, with fights that quicken the pulse, with comedy that provokes unstoppable laughter – you honour his true intent by creating theatre that doesn't just engage the mind but seizes the whole person.

This is the theatre that sends even the most reluctant audience member home saying, against all expectations, *That was bloody good*. There is no higher compliment. That's the kind of word-of-mouth that sells tickets, because you've genuinely *affected* the audience.

This is the essence of Bloody Good Shakespeare: theatre that pulses with life and refuses to let audiences remain passive. It's Shakespeare unleashed and unchained from reverent whispers and dusty scholarship. In the Renaissance playhouse, audiences didn't silently watch intellectual concepts, they collaborated in the performance. Shakespeare wrote for this electric atmosphere, this communion between actor and audience, this shared breath and heartbeat.

Shakespeare sucks

Let's face it: most people think Shakespeare sucks. Too boring. Too dense. Too dusty. Too dead. And honestly? Most productions prove them right. They're timid. Bloodless. Embalmed in reverence. Shakespeare as museum artefact. Shakespeare as PhD thesis.

Add to that the modern judgments. Sexist. Racist. Imperialist. 'Pale, male, and stale.' Ouch. It's no wonder young audiences turn away. Why should they care about a dead white guy propped up by school exams and academic guilt?

But here's the thing: that's not Shakespeare. Not the one I know. Not the one who packed theatres with thousands, wrote for a rowdy, living audience, and created characters who feel more alive than most people you meet on the street.

The plays aren't boring. But academics and some theatremakers can be. Shakespeare designed most of his plays to be drenched in shared light. We entomb them in darkness. Drain them of joy. Speak them like scripture. Forget the audience is even there.

As for the charges – sexism, racism, colonialism – yes, those legacies cling to the world that made him. But Shakespeare himself is slippery. It's hard to find the man himself in his work. There's no doubt that some of Shakespeare's characters are sexist, or racist, or just plain horrible. But this does not mean that Shakespeare's work is those things, or that Shakespeare himself was or is sexist, racist or imperialist.

In fact, I think you'd be hard pressed to find a more enlightened Jacobean.

Somewhere along the way, directors became convinced that Shakespeare must be reinvented to be interesting, or apologised for to be acceptable. This leads to productions buried under heavy-handed concepts that drown the play rather than elevate it. The audience spends half the evening trying to decipher why Hamlet is a hedge fund manager or why the witches in *Macbeth* are dressed as corporate executives.

The problem isn't that Shakespeare can't withstand bold ideas, because he absolutely can. The problem is that these heavy concepts can be substitutes for actually performing the story as written. Sometimes I can't help but feel they're a cop out for directors who are insecure about their ability to direct Shakespeare in a way that will grip the audience. The reasoning seems to be that the play will be boring, but at least the concept can be interesting. Sadly, concepts are often like lectures. They are academically interesting, but fail in performance. Perhaps they are, in the words of the old phrase, honey as a sauce to sugar.

Because theatre should never feel like a lecture. Audiences don't go to the theatre to be scolded or to endure a night of self-important messaging. If you want your work to be seen by more than just your echo chamber, you need to appeal to the widest possible audience.

That means telling the story as Shakespeare wrote it first, not using theatre as a vehicle for fashionable political causes or propaganda.

Shakespeare's plays already tackle power, gender, justice, love, and ambition with nuance and depth. Theatremakers must trust that the audience are smart enough to see the endless parallels between our modern world and Shakespeare's own. And they will, if you don't bore them to death first.

Shakespeare that sucks is Shakespeare that forgets to entertain. It is Shakespeare that gets lost in its own self-importance, that values theory over thrill, that treats the audience as passive rather than essential.

This sort of Shakespeare is like a boring guest at a party, who, thinking that they are totally fascinating, talks about themselves all night and never asks you a single question.

But when Shakespeare is done right, when it's a conversation not a monologue, when it forges a deep connection with the audience, when it's allowed to be as bloody, spectacular, hilarious, and heartbreaking as it was meant to be, it reminds us why these plays have survived for centuries.

It's not because they are artifacts of literary genius. It's because they are still, when freed from the weight of bad decisions, bloody good theatre.

Audiences don't want safe, dusty, polite Shakespeare. They want theatre that makes them *lean forward*. That grips them by the collar. That reminds them what it means to be *alive, in a shared space, experiencing something unique and unifying with actors and strangers alike.*

I know this because I've spent my career fighting for it. I've proved beyond doubt that when you stage Shakespeare as he was meant to be staged, audiences come in droves. Because they don't want to miss out on a thrilling, unforgettable experience.

The core principles of Bloody Good Shakespeare

If you want to make your audiences fall in love with Shakespeare, strip away the fluff and start with four core principles. These are sharp tools forged in the crucible of live performance: practical, deceptively simple, and battle-tested in front of hundreds of thousands of audience members. Get these right, and everything else will take care of itself.

1. Humour: Make 'em laugh, make 'em cry

Let's be clear. If Shakespeare's plays weren't both hugely funny and deeply moving, they wouldn't have survived. That's the reason why his plays were a smash hit in those large public theatres in the first place. The myth of Shakespeare as lofty, literary, and solemn is just that – a myth.

His audiences came for a good time. They wanted rude jokes, love triangles, slapstick, sword fights, ghosts, mistaken identities, and the kind of biting wit that could bring the house down.

Over the centuries, some of his humour has dated, and some we miss because we're no longer looking for it or expecting it. But the plays are full of unexpected humour, and too often this is neglected, overlooked, or even cut because at first glance it looks like it won't land with modern audiences.

Humour is the engine of connection. It opens the audience. It makes them listen, desperate not to miss a laugh. And when the hammer of tragedy inevitably falls, it hits a thousand times harder because they've let their guard down.

Look at the great tragedies: Hamlet breaks tension with gravediggers who joke about death. King Lear has his Fool, who speaks truth through comedy. *Macbeth* has a porter who stumbles onstage, drunk, just moments after a brutal murder. These moments are deliberate and structural. They keep the audience with you. They keep the play alive.

And the comedies? They're full of heartbreak. *Much Ado About Nothing* dances on the edge of a funeral. *Twelfth Night* begins with a deadly shipwreck and ends with a broken heart. *The Comedy of Errors* starts with a father facing death and ends with a long-lost family reunited. Beneath the jokes is real human pain. Without it, the comedy rings hollow.

So let the laughter live right alongside the tears. Play both, hard. Make them roar with laughter and then shatter their hearts in the next beat. That's Shakespeare's rhythm. That's the balance that keeps audiences rapt. That's what fills theatres.

2. Direct address: Make theatre *with* the audience, not *at* them

In most modern theatre, the audience sits in the dark. Invisible. Silent. Ignored. Actors stare past them into the void. But Shakespeare didn't write for that theatre. He wrote for a crowd in broad daylight, packed in close, reacting out loud. He wrote for a stage that demanded the actor see the audience, and make the play with them by speaking directly to them.

Direct address is the lifeblood of Shakespeare's performance style. In total contrast to modern naturalistic theatre, Shakespeare is written to be spoken directly to the audience, face to face. To draw them in as collaborators in the making of the story.

Every soliloquy is a dialogue. Every line is the opportunity for true connection. The audience must not be a passive spectator. They must participate. As confidants. As allies. As dear friends. As enemies. They're every bit as alive in the moment as the actors.

This means as an actor you must look them in the eyes. Sustain the moment. Speak to them. Feel their energy and use it.

When you involve the audience, they become co-creators. They carry the play with you. And every single performance becomes unique. No two shows are the same. Because no two audiences are the same. That is the magic of live theatre. That is, fundamentally, *the point*.

This is ancient. It is powerful. It creates the immediacy that modern audiences crave. It restores the intimacy and danger that made Shakespeare's plays electric. Repeat after me: *There is no fourth wall in Shakespeare.*

3. Spectacle: If you can do it live, do it big

Shakespeare's theatre was full of spectacle. His stage directions are clear: storms, ghosts, battles, banquets, weddings, suicides, stabbings, beheadings, births, betrayals, storms, and magic. It was a feast for the senses. His theatre was spectacular and deeply visceral.

Spectacle with emotion is incredibly powerful stuff. It jolts audiences awake. It physically affects their body. It gives them a sense that the production is expanding, unpredictable. It is theatrical gold.

If someone dies, show us the death. If someone is crowned, let us see the crown. Use real blood. Real steel. Real sweat. Use fire. Use live music, thunder, smoke, sword fights, flying rigs. Let the audience feel it in their bones.

But you must always serve the story. It's not about dazzling for the sake of it. It's about immersion. It's about amplification. Every cannon blast, every choreographed brawl, every ghostly entrance must push the story deeper into the hearts of the audience.

And don't ever hide behind pre-recorded digital trickery. If it can be done live – do it live. That's the magic of theatre. The risk. The sweat. The breath. The moment of *Oh God, that could go wrong*. That's what hooks an audience.

Modern audiences are saturated with screens. They've seen CGI armies and perfect edits. But they're unlikely to have seen a man bleeding to death five feet from their face, or heard the sound of a broadsword striking a steel helmet just inches away.

4. Courage: The principle that frees the others

To those first three simple principles, I add a fourth. Courage.

To make theatre like this – to really make Shakespeare that lives – you need courage.

Courage means making bold choices. It means risking failure. It means confronting the darkest parts of the human condition, because that's where Shakespeare excels. He didn't flinch from power, or violence, or race, or sex, or death. Neither should we.

In our current climate, it's easy to be afraid. Afraid of controversy. Afraid of backlash. Afraid of getting it wrong. But fear is the enemy of art. Sanitised Shakespeare is a betrayal. If it doesn't provoke, it isn't doing its job.

You need the courage to trust the text. To speak plainly. To cut fearlessly. To embrace the play's contradictions and rough edges. As a director, you must be willing to push your actors – and yourself – beyond what feels comfortable. As an actor, you must be ready to go all in.

Courage doesn't mean certainty. It means conviction in the face of doubt. Some risks will fail. Some bold choices won't land. That's okay. Audiences can forgive failure. What they will not forgive is cowardice.

When you dare greatly, you give permission. To your cast. To your crew. To your audience. You create a space where truth can happen. So let courage lead. Let it be the spine of your work. Let it shape your humour, your address, your spectacle. And when it all comes together, when the risk pays off, something extraordinary will happen. The theatre you make will be of such power that the audience will remember it for the rest of their lives.

These four principles – Humour, Direct Address, Spectacle, and Courage – are the bedrock of Bloody Good Shakespeare. Master these, and you're no longer staging a play. You're crafting an experience. One that grabs your audience by the throat, shakes them by the soul, and leaves them transformed forever.

We're all in this together

The Pop-up Globe experiment proved what many had forgotten: Shakespeare can still be wildly popular. We demonstrated that when his plays are performed with immediacy, audience connection, powerful acting, purposeful spectacle, and courage, they remain the most vital theatre on the planet.

As our digital lives become increasingly isolated, theatre-makers must boldly reclaim theatre's identity as a human event – a gathering, a celebration, a ritual – by leaning into what makes it irreplaceable: its liveness, its risk, its communion.

My hope is that through this book, more theatre will be made – not just more Shakespeare, but better Shakespeare. Bolder Shakespeare. Bloodier Shakespeare. Theatre that matters. Theatre that changes lives. Theatre that reminds us, in a world increasingly defined by digital detachment, what it means to be human.

The game's afoot. Let's play.

Play, Space, Company

IF YOU WANT TO work with the greatest playwright in English-speaking history, you need a vision.

You need to answer the age-old producer's questions: *why this play, in this space, with these actors, now?* Be ambitious. Undertaking a 'safe', small-scale production will use exactly the same amount of emotional energy as creating something at the edge of what you believe to be possible. An ambitious shared vision, that brings a company along with it, will take you to remarkable places.

You presumably want as many people as possible to see your work on stage. You may already have a company to work with, or perhaps you have been asked to direct for someone else's company. Perhaps you are starting from scratch, in which case you will need to assemble the actors yourself. However you are working, the first and most important thing to do is to decide which play you will perform.

Play

The choice of play is everything. Before a single line is spoken, before an actor sets foot on stage, before the first ticket is sold, the play itself determines the path ahead. It dictates the energy of the production, the type of audience it will attract, and, crucially, the venue in which it must be staged. A great production begins with the right play, chosen for the right reasons, at the right moment in time. But choosing wisely is no small task – it requires a deep understanding of the play's potential to resonate with audiences, its ability to thrive in the chosen space, and its capacity to stir something important and necessary within the cultural moment.

Some of Shakespeare's plays are always popular. *Romeo and Juliet*, *Much Ado About Nothing*, *A Midsummer Night's Dream*, *Macbeth* – these plays need no justification. Their names alone draw some audiences, their stories are deeply embedded in our cultural consciousness, and their themes resonate across generations. Choosing one of these plays is never a mistake; the challenge lies in ensuring that you are prepared to meet the technical demands. Blood, war, witches, duels, fairies. They must all be spectacular.

Audiences come to these plays with expectations. They want *Romeo and Juliet* to be breathtakingly romantic, they want *Much Ado About Nothing* to be joyous and witty, and they want *Macbeth* to chill them to the bone. The director's task is to honour these expectations while also exceeding them – bringing something more, something surprising to the table. The greatest danger in staging these plays is complacency; the assumption that they will work simply because they are beloved.

Beyond the ever-popular works, there is another category of Shakespeare's plays – those that rise and fall in relevance depending on the world we live in. At any given moment, two or three Shakespeare plays bring our contemporary world into focus with piercing clarity. When Donald Trump was first elected, *Julius Caesar* became the Shakespeare play of the moment – its exploration of power, populism, and political violence suddenly felt dangerously immediate. When the #MeToo movement spread across the world, *Measure for Measure* emerged as a vital theatrical response – its themes of sexual coercion, power dynamics, and institutional corruption striking with renewed force.

This is why the choice of play must be made with absolute care. It should be guided by two crucial factors: *the popularity of the text* and *the immediacy of its themes*. A director must not simply ask, *What play do I want to direct?* but *What play needs to be staged right now?* This is the difference between vanity and vision. A truly great production does not exist in isolation – it is in conversation with its audience, with the world beyond the theatre walls.

There is no point in trying to attract thousands of audience members to *Timon of Athens* – unless you already have a passionate, loyal audience that trusts you. Some plays require too much of an uphill battle to market to the general public, and in an era when competition for attention is fiercer than ever, a production that fails to excite from the outset is already doomed. This is not about dumbing down the work or avoiding risk. It is about acknowledging that some plays come with built-in appeal, while others demand a long, patient journey to bring them into the public eye.

If you can, choose two plays and make them both at the same time with the same actors. Repertory theatre is one of the most effective ways to maximise audience reach and deepen engagement. It's also the way that Shakespeare's own company worked. In the repertory model, one cast performs two (or more!) productions in alternation – an approach that costs only a little more but allows for an increase in audience attendance. Many who see one production will return to see the other, particularly if the two plays are programmed to complement or contrast with each other in theme and tone, and special ticket packages are offered to entice them.

Repertory theatre allows actors to develop richer performances, as their work in one play informs their approach to the other. It fosters a sense of continuity and discovery for the audience, who experience the same actors inhabiting different roles, revealing their talent and versatility.

Furthermore, repertory theatre encourages artistic innovation. Directors and actors must find ways to differentiate each production while keeping a consistent performance energy. If one play is a comedy and the other a tragedy, this juxtaposition deepens the audience's appreciation of Shakespeare's range. A production of *Twelfth Night* may reveal nuances that only become apparent when performed alongside *King Lear*. The contrast enriches both plays, making the audience's experience fuller and more rewarding.

Shakespeare gives us a vast landscape of human experience, but it is up to us to decide which paths to explore. So choose with the knowledge that Shakespeare's plays do not belong to the past. They belong to *now*. They belong to the audience, to the cultural moment, to the shared experience of actors and spectators alike. This is why Shakespeare will always be our contemporary: because his plays reflect both Shakespeare's world, and our own, simultaneously. When the choice of play, the immediacy of its themes, and the resonance of its performance space align – then the theatre becomes something greater than itself. It becomes an event, a conversation, an unforgettable encounter between past and present, between actor and audience, between story and reality.

But choosing the right play is only the beginning. The next crucial step is to truly know the play you have chosen – not merely the version that sits in modern editions, but to get as close as possible to the play as Shakespeare wrote it. Once you've selected your play, you must do your research to re-connect with the raw material of Shakespeare's theatrical imagination.

The truth is, most of us encounter Shakespeare in versions that have been tampered with, altered, reshaped by editors over centuries. What you hold in your hands is often the work of many hands – not just his. Some plays exist in multiple versions, quartos and folios that don't always agree. If you want to understand Shakespeare, go back. Read the Folio, the quartos. Look at the original spelling, the punctuation, the shape of the text.

As a director, I don't trust modern editions. I go back to the earliest editions I can find and write the script out myself, word by word. Before the actors even speak, I have already lived the language and made my own choices about every element that is left in place – or removed.

To do this is to place yourself in direct conversation with the text. To forge a personal relationship with Shakespeare himself. The process of copying out a play line by line is not a passive one. It forces you to slow down, to see the choices that have been made by editors, to question why a certain word is there, to feel the weight of the language in your own hand. It is an act of ownership, of engagement. It is the first rehearsal before the actors have even arrived. You come to know the text in a way that a simple read-through will never allow.

Space

Once upon a time, Shakespeare and his contemporaries built new spaces to stage their works. This was the birth of modern theatre, an art form that flourished in spaces designed to unite actor and audience. These theatres, one of which was the original Globe, were places of immediacy and energy, where plays were not simply performed but *experienced*. Shakespeare's work was immensely popular, drawing crowds from all walks of life. The structure of the playhouses themselves – open to the elements, with a thrust stage extending into the audience – demanded a dynamic, direct style of performance that remains unparalleled in its vitality.

Shakespeare's company performed on a fixed, unchanging platform that became the equivalent of having no set at all. In daylight, with actors fully visible, their expressions readable from every tier of the theatre. When performances moved indoors, the lighting was provided by candles: flickering, uneven, nothing like the precise, controlled stage lighting of today. All music was played live, immediate and responsive. In the huge open-air amphitheatres of the Globe and the Rose, the audience stood, pressed close, which must have naturally limited performance length to three hours or so at most.

These theatres were generally extremely popular – and profitable. They became institutions, with famous resident companies working with equally famous playwrights who wrote plays with the sole purpose of being performed on that stage, in that space. It was the first golden age of English-speaking theatre.

Then, history intervened. The open-air theatres were closed at the Civil War in 1642 and later demolished. After the 1660 Restoration, a new kind of theatre emerged; indoors, with lit stages, elaborate sets and a different relationship between actor and audience. This transformation reshaped the nature of performance, slowly distancing actors from their audiences. Theatre thrived in these surroundings for nearly two hundred years, evolving into the grand institutions of the eighteenth and nineteenth centuries.

Then directors and practitioners took practical steps to return his plays to their original performance conditions. This movement, originating in the 1890s with William Poel, has continued to evolve. Pop-up Globe, Shakespeare's Globe in London, and the many other replica Globes around the world are part of this ongoing modern exploration. The insatiable hunger for unobtainable authenticity, for the feeling of encountering Shakespeare's work as his first audiences did, is a force that has shaped theatre for generations.

After the Second World War, another seismic shift occurred. The tumult of the 1960s brought about the studio theatre movement. The black box theatre was born: intimate, stripped back, and flexible. By rejecting elaborate sets in favor of minimalist, flexible staging, directors like Peter Brook and Trevor Nunn fostered greater audience intimacy, spontaneity, and innovation. The Royal Shakespeare Company's studio theatre, The Other Place, exemplified this new impulse, a radical departure from the proscenium arch theatres that had dominated for centuries. For forty years, classical theatre thrived in these smaller, more intimate venues.

But now, everything has changed again. The most interesting theatre is no longer confined to theatres at all. The most thrilling Shakespeare is being staged in found spaces, or in purpose-built environments designed to create an event beyond the play itself. *Measure for Measure* staged in an abandoned prison. *Macbeth* in the tunnels beneath a fourteenth century castle. Pop-up Globe. Productions set in warehouses, derelict churches, town squares. These performances exist not just as plays but as experiences, drawing audiences as much for the space as for the production itself. The impact of a performance is now inseparable from its setting. These choices are no accident. They are a conscious effort to enhance storytelling by immersing the audience in a world beyond the stage.

This shift is part of the modern experience economy. Just as in Shakespeare's time, today's audiences seek more than just a show; they want an *event*. They want to feel they are part of something singular, something they will never see again. They are drawn to the mystery of a hidden location, the excitement of stepping into an unfamiliar space. The venue itself is a vital character in the production. But this comes with a warning: no audience will forgive a production that does not match the promise of the setting. The space may lure them in, but the storytelling must captivate them. The venue and the production must work together, each enhancing the other. The right space should amplify the story, adding a new dimension to the audience's engagement.

In this new era, the best Shakespeare productions do not *fit* into conventional spaces, they *create* their own. The lesson from Shakespeare's own time is clear: if the right space does not exist, build it. Pop-up Globe proved this. By reconstructing a Jacobean playhouse, it demonstrated the power of staging Shakespeare in the conditions for which it was written. Audiences responded to the thrill of shared light, of actors addressing them directly, of a space that encouraged participation rather than passive observation. The space shaped the performances, and the performances, in turn, defined the space.

Finding or building your perfect performance space opens your production to new audiences. There are many people who will never step foot into a traditional theatre. Sadly, they feel that such a space is 'not for the likes of them'. This is why I made a huge amount of open air theatre for the first ten years of my professional career. There is a different, new audience for such work. If the people will not come to the theatre, the theatre must go to them.

Some weeks after the first Pop-up Globe opened, I was walking across a square by the theatre in central Auckland. I bumped into a well-known aficionado of New Zealand theatre, someone I hadn't seen for over a year. He asked me how Pop-up Globe was going. I said, *well, we've sold 50,000 tickets.* He sniffed. *It's just a gimmick*, he said, *but a good one.*

Was he right? I thought about this for a long time. Pop-up Globe with poor performances would indeed have been a gimmick – a fancy temporary structure with 'tourist' Shakespeare on stage. But with passionate, innovative performances, it certainly couldn't be called just a gimmick. As we went on to sell another 700,000 tickets, I think I was right. The moral? There's nothing wrong with theatre that starts as a gimmick – if it proves itself as something greater. A bold idea may be what draws people in, but it is the work itself that keeps them coming back. The spectacle, the setting, the concept – all of these must ultimately serve the play.

Theatre-makers should not fear spectacle, or being dismissed as a 'gimmick'. What they should fear are empty seats caused by productions that do not justify their setting, that waste the opportunities presented by their chosen space. Pop-up Globe was not about nostalgia; it was about discovery. It was a challenge to both actors and audiences to rethink what Shakespeare could be. The same applies to any modern production staged in an unconventional setting. A great venue alone is not enough.

To stage truly popular Shakespeare, directors and producers must think beyond the play itself. They must ask: *Where should this story be told? What space will amplify its themes, heighten its impact? How do we make this an event, rather than just a performance?* The answers to these questions will define the next great wave of Shakespearean theatre. A great venue does not merely house a performance; it enhances it, making it an event, an experience, a moment that lingers in memory. Spaces where theatre is not just seen but *felt.*

The ideal Shakespearean production starts with a universally lit, large, open, thrust stage space, surrounded on three sides by an audience that is visible to the actors and close enough to touch them. Live music only, no amplification, no microphones. A single, unchanging set. No fourth wall.

The audience must be physically included. Entrances and exits through the audience create surprise and opportunities for interplay. Scenes that unfold in the midst of the audience rather than in front of them, or in a dialogue between actors on stage and actors amongst the crowd. The audience must be spoken to, acknowledged, absorbed into the world of the play. Shakespeare is a space of interaction, where the actors and the audience share breath, energy, the same flickering moment in time.

This demands big stage playing areas – expansive, unencumbered, ideally a stage of at least 100 square metres. It demands a cast large enough to populate that space fully. Eight actors would be a minimum; twelve to fifteen, including musicians, is ideal. Theatre is at its best when the stage is always in motion, when movement flows seamlessly from one moment to the next. Shakespeare's plays thrive on rhythm, on pace, on momentum, and nothing should be allowed to slow that.

Make theatre for the people. Everyone. The best Shakespearean productions should not be exclusive, locked behind high ticket prices and reserved for an elite audience. There must be tickets priced at the cost of a couple of cups of coffee – low enough that anyone can take a chance on an evening of Shakespeare.

At the same time, there must be premium seating, tickets ten or twenty times the price, ensuring the financial sustainability of the production while keeping it open to all. It took me a long time to learn that some people *want to pay more*. The experience should feel democratic, immediate, available to anyone willing to step into the world of the play, whatever the size of their wallet.

Making Shakespeare work in proscenium spaces

While Pop-up Globe was purpose-built for Shakespeare, it remains a fact that many productions today take place in traditional proscenium arch theatres. If you must use a proscenium theatre (and I urge you not to), how do we maintain the principles of immediacy, connection, and energy in these spaces? You must embrace simplicity and restructure the audience relationship.

1. One fixed set

A single, versatile backdrop that can serve as the setting for any scene removes the need for elaborate scene changes, ensuring the play moves at full pace. Shakespeare's words create the world – there's no need to shift vast pieces of scenery to reinforce that. A multi-level structure with entrances at different heights can provide flexibility while maintaining speed and fluidity.

2. Universal lighting

Actors and audience should be lit together as much as possible. This maintains a sense of shared space, preventing actors from performing into a void. The audience must feel seen, allowing for a dynamic relationship between performers and spectators. If full shared light isn't possible, keeping the audience in low light rather than total darkness ensures they remain an active part of the event rather than passive observers.

3. Extending the stage

Ideally, a thrust stage should be built over the stalls, bringing the actors into the audience's space. If this isn't possible, the minimum requirement should be audience seating on stage. Having spectators on stage transforms the dynamic – actors have people to play off, just as they did in Shakespeare's time. Wherever possible, performers should break free from the proscenium and engage directly with the audience – using the aisles, balconies, or any available space. Hide amongst them. Treat them as a mob to be roused. Be inventive. Surprise them.

4. Stripping back technology

Shakespeare doesn't need cinematic lighting cues or automated scenery. The simpler the setup, the more time is spent in rehearsals working on what truly matters: the performances. Sound effects and music should be live whenever possible – this creates a richer, more organic theatrical experience. Keep it simple, keep it live.

5. Using direct address and rethinking blocking

We'll return to direct address later, but the audience must be included in the storytelling. A proscenium arch stage naturally directs all focus forward, but this doesn't mean actors should remain locked in a presentational mode. Encourage movement that breaks traditional frontal staging – have actors turn outward to play to different sections of the audience, move into the aisles, or position themselves in ways that keep the space alive. Eye contact and direct address become even more crucial in this setup, ensuring the audience remains engaged.

As theatre continues to evolve, one thing remains constant: Shakespeare's plays are astonishingly adaptable. They were never meant to be locked in one form, one venue, one way of being performed. His plays were originally presented at the monarch's court, in the freezing halls of Jacobean country houses, in the indoor theatre at Blackfriars, and on the stages of the open-air London playhouses. They have survived for over 400 years because they change with the times.

The challenge for today's theatre-makers is to harness that adaptability, to push boundaries, to create experiences that audiences will never forget. And if that means building new theatres, reclaiming old ones, or staging plays in places never before considered in order to introduce new audiences to Shakespeare – then so be it.

Company

Shakespeare did not create his plays to be enjoyed in solitude as English Literature. They were made for his company – a living, breathing, tightly bonded group of players who worked together, night after night, to bring stories to life.

A Shakespeare theatre company is unlike anything else. Unlike many drama theatre companies, it is usually a large company, with a dozen or more actors, musicians and creatives. It is a family, a community, debating chamber, a place of trust and passion, of laughter and intense physical effort. It is a structure built not on bricks and mortar, but on the bonds between its members.

And the first brick in that invisible structure is casting. Casting is an act of vision, drawn from your understanding of the play you have chosen. Done well, it lays the foundation for everything to follow.

When casting, the director's chief duty is to the story. If the audience cannot tell who is who, what is happening, and why, then the production has already failed. The plays are linguistically demanding. We do not need to make them harder by casting in ways that confuse.

Cast on merit first. Always. Choose those with the skill, presence, and attitude to carry the line and the moment. Choose those who connect. But remember also that talent is not born equal, it emerges where it is allowed to emerge. I always hold open auditions in order to welcome those from outside the usual circles and to show in action that anyone is welcome to throw their hat into the ring. And unless there are strong artistic reasons for casting otherwise, it makes good sense for the company to roughly represent the likely demographic of the audience – broadly, without quotas or slogans. Representation matters, but it must serve Shakespeare's story.

But merit alone is not enough. The actor must also fit the company. No prima donnas. No egos that sour the room. Shakespearean rehearsal rooms are intensive, intimate, and long-lived. Even one difficult presence can poison the dynamic. So when you're casting, don't rely solely on the audition. Try to meet the actor for a coffee or a walk. Listen. Observe. Will this person work well with others? Will they pull their weight? Will they lift the room or drain it? Cast not only for talent, but for temperament. A company is not a collection of stars, it must be a single, beating heart.

Gender casting requires particular care. Shakespeare's company was all male. The canon leans heavily toward male roles. Demanding a balanced 50/50 gender split is often neither possible nor truthful. Gender-bending can work. Done right, it clarifies. Done wrong, it alienates. Audiences are often more conservative than artists care to admit. Take them with you. Don't preach at them – lead them.

Tom Mallaburn's 2017 *As You Like It* at Pop-up Globe reimagined Phoebe as Phoebus, a handsome and vain young man pursued by Silvius. The same-sex love story emerged naturally from the text of the play, already steeped in cross-dressing and gender confusion. The result felt honest and precise. In Melbourne, where the production coincided with national debate on marriage equality, it struck a deep chord, creating a timely echo between the playhouse and the people.

Rita Stone's 2018 *Julius Caesar*, by contrast, reversed gender across the board. Women held the reins of power. Men stayed at home. The world was matriarchal, merciless, cold. The timing helped. Jacinda Ardern led New Zealand, and Theresa May led Britain. Audiences recognised the moment. There was an electricity to the production because it reflected the world around it.

These examples succeeded because they started with the story. That is the challenging task before you, to tell the story and serve the play. It's wise to do everything you can at the casting stage to make the story you plan to tell as clear and easy to follow as possible.

At Pop-up Globe, we began with one all-male and one mixed-gender company, not out of dogma, but because we were making theatre in a replica of Shakespeare's own theatre, replicating not only its architecture but many of the conditions of its performance style. I had never directed all-male casts before, and found it theatrically fascinating. Later, we expanded to three companies: one all-male, one mixed-gender, and one reverse-gendered. This gave a rough 50/50 gender balance across five productions running in repertory. In 2018, following criticism from some in the arts community and wide consultation with our company, we adopted a 50/50 gender casting policy across the company (but not the individual productions) in each season. While I have reservations about quota-based approaches, preferring to cast according to the artistic aims of the company or production, once the decision was made, we embraced it – and made some of our best work. Ultimately, what matters most is not the gender or ethnicity of the actors, but the collective act of working together to create compelling theatre that transports audiences from their daily lives into a realm of possibility and wonder.

However you plan to stage the production, once casting is complete, the true work begins: forging the cast into a company. Individual excellence must now give way to collective purpose. To make exciting, gripping Shakespeare, the company must become more than the sum of its parts, it must develop a shared language, a shared rhythm, a shared will to make meaning together.

Shakespeare's own company, the Lord Chamberlain's Men, later called the King's Men, was a collective of extraordinary talent, bound by mutual trust and the shared goal of creating powerful theatre. The importance of this company is shown by the decision to list the core members in the opening pages of the 1623 Folio. Their strength lay not just in individual brilliance but in their unity, their belief in each other, and in their commitment to working together over many years. This is what creates morale: professionalism, resilience, commitment to excellence, a shared vision that stands the test of time.

Morale in a theatre company is not a static thing. It rises, falls, surges, and collapses in great waves, pulled by the tides of triumph and exhaustion, by the weight of expectation and the fire of creation. In a company as ambitious, as physically and emotionally demanding as Pop-up Globe, morale was everything. It was the invisible force that kept the company together even in the most difficult times. With good morale, anything is possible. Where morale is poor, even the simplest things can become impossible.

At its best, it was pure camaraderie, the reckless joy of knowing that we were all in the same madness together. The company grew so rapidly – three people became over one hundred in two months, then quickly scaled again a year or so later to around 250 – and that sudden expansion created both chaos and a kind of breathless excitement. The scale of it was staggering. At times, it felt like an impossible machine, driven by adrenaline and sheer belief.

And yet, in that whirlwind, the company found its rhythm. The actors, the costume makers, the marketing team, the armourers, the stagehands, the front-of-house team, the volunteer ushers – each had a part to play, each was vital. That sense of shared purpose, that *this thing must happen and we are the ones making it happen*, carried us through the most impossible days.

It was not always easy. The exhaustion was real. There were days when the long hours, the relentless pace, and the sheer physicality of the work pushed people to their limits. But still the company held – pulling together in adversity rather than ripping apart. The backstage area at our Auckland playhouse flooded in extreme conditions: I arrived to discover actors and stage managers stripped to the waist, working together to bail out the water. In Perth, a severe afternoon storm whipped up and threatened the integrity of the playhouse mid-dress rehearsal: the company decamped to a local fast food joint in full costume, played music and sang. A severe electrical storm struck the Sydney Pop-up Globe on the opening night of *The Merchant of Venice*. The playhouse was actually struck by lightning during one of the later scenes with a very audible bang. The company paused, ad libbed about this 'electrifying moment', and carried on.

A theatre in constant motion – a pop-up space, built and dismantled, shifting locations, crossing borders – meant there was never a true sense of stillness. We rehearsed in one space, performed in another, packed up and did it again. Broken legs, sudden illnesses resulted in understudies or directors going on at the last moment to cover. High pressure stuff. And yet, for all of it, the morale of the company was astonishing. There was a shared understanding that what we were doing *mattered*. That we were not simply performing Shakespeare, but making something alive, something life-changing, something our audiences had never seen before.

But morale is fragile. As much as it thrives on energy and success, it can also be crushed by doubt, by exhaustion, by the slow grind of repetition. The danger of a long run is that what once felt thrilling can start to feel like a routine. Actors are not machines, and nor are creatives.

There were times, deep into a season, when even the most dedicated among us felt the weight of it. The trick – the essential skill of any great company – is knowing how to keep the fire alive. It is about leadership, about trust, about understanding that morale is not simply about making people feel good, but about making them understand that they are *necessary*.

Pop-up Globe, in its best moments, achieved that. The company was an ecosystem, each part feeding the other. The actors thrived on the response of the audience, the crew fed off the energy of the performances, and the sense of *making history* – that this was not just another show, but something larger – kept it all moving. And yet, it was also about care. About knowing when to push and when to pull back. About recognising that even the most committed performer has limits.

I think of the moments when exhaustion nearly broke us. The nights when rain lashed against the theatre, when the wind howled, when the stage was slick and treacherous, and yet the audience stayed. We could see their faces, upturned, soaked, unwilling to leave. Those were the moments that reminded the company why they did this. Because theatre, real theatre, is not about comfort. It is about connection. About the unrepeatable alchemy of *this night, this audience, this performance*. And for all the fatigue, for all the bruises, for all the sheer grind of it – those moments were worth it.

There is something about working in a company like this that bonds people in a way nothing else does. It is not like film, where scenes are shot and reshot, where actors disappear into trailers between takes. It is not like conventional theatre, where actors retreat to dressing rooms, separated from the crowd. Pop-up Globe had a rawness to it, a sense of exposure, because the actors were always within clear earshot of the stage, even at rest. The noise from the audience during a performance was so loud that it could be heard from two hundred metres away. The audience was *there*, inescapable, part of the world of the play. And that changed everything. It meant that every night was different, that no performance could be mechanical, that every reaction mattered.

I have seen actors lifted by that, transformed by it. I have seen actors who, only moments before, had been slumped in exhaustion in the green room step onto that stage and *ignite*. Because the energy of the crowd, the energy of the company, pulled them forward. And I have seen the opposite – I have seen actors retreat into themselves, struggle under the weight of it. It happens. It is inevitable. The job of a great company is to collectively carry our people, to hold them until they find their footing again.

Morale extends beyond the actors. It is one thing to direct a play as a freelance director. To step into the rehearsal room, script in hand, and shape performances, guide actors, carve meaning from centuries-old text, then leave again for the next gig. It is another thing entirely to form a company, to produce and direct the work, to build the damn theatre from scratch, to carry it all – the vision, the finances, the responsibilities, the crises – on your back. And yet, for directors with their own company, this must be your life. A director, yes, but also a producer, a leader, an entrepreneur, a fire-fighter, a strategist, a marketer, even an occasional therapist.

There will be long nights when sleep will be an afterthought, and exhaustion becomes a constant companion. In those hours, the weight of leadership can be suffocating. Every financial decision can feel like a gamble, every production choice a battle between art and survival.

I remember sitting in our offices, staring at the numbers, knowing that if one deal fell through, if one tour flopped, everything would come crashing down. But even in those moments, there was never an option to stop. The machine has to keep moving.

And yet, in the midst of that chaos, there will be moments of sheer, undeniable magic. The first performance of *Twelfth Night*, where the audience laughed so freely, so unexpectedly, that the actors had to hold for the sound. Watching Chris Huntly-Turner as Henry V in a tropical storm, keeping the audience in the palm of his hand as the rain poured down.

But theatre is not just moments – it is a vast convulsive effort by a unified team. It is the endless, grinding work that no audience ever sees. The die-hard wardrobe team, washing blood from costumes and oiling armour late into the night. The crew arriving before dawn to fix a prop that splintered the night before. The marketing team rewriting campaigns at midnight to boost ticket sales. The actors pushing through illness, exhaustion, the weight of performing the same words night after night, knowing that for someone in the audience, it was always the first time.

It was not an easy company to be part of. It was demanding, relentless, at times utterly mad. But for those who were there, who stood on that stage and felt the charge of it, who looked out at an audience that *wanted* to be part of it all – there was nothing else like it. Nothing else that could match the sheer, undeniable, living force of it.

And that, more than anything, is what keeps morale alive. Not comfort. Not ease. But the knowledge that what you are doing is hard, but vital. That it will never be like this again. That this, right now, is the moment. And you – the whole company, together – are in it together.

In 2018, after years of working at breakneck pace – under intense public scrutiny and through moments of real pain and trauma that bound our company together like a family – I distilled our shared experience into three guiding principles: **Unity, Hope, and Joy**.

These weren't abstract ideals. They were the living foundation of our company culture. I spoke about them at every major company meeting. We put them on the walls of our offices and rehearsal rooms. And I asked every member of the company to reflect on their choices – on and off the stage – by asking a simple question: *Does my action bring Unity, Hope, or Joy? Or does it bring the opposite?* That was the test.

And these principles aren't just for theatre. They're universal. You'll find them at the heart of every great team.

Unity, not division. A company must move as one, bound by a shared purpose. Rivalries and egos have no place where true collaboration is needed. When the actors trust one another – when they know that they are held by the company – the stage becomes a space of limitless possibility. The audience feels it, too. They sense the connection between players, the deep, unspoken trust, and it draws them in.

Hope, not despair. Theatre, at its best, offers a vision of what is possible. The director must instill this belief in the company – that no matter the obstacles, no matter the challenges, the work will be achieved, and it will be extraordinary. Rehearsals must be places of exploration, not fear; of problem-solving, not criticism. This sense of shared hope is what carries a production from first read-through to opening night.

Joy, not misery. The best theatre is made with joy, and that's just as it should be. Even in the darkest tragedies, there must be exhilaration in the act of performance. Rehearsals should be filled with laughter, with passionate debate, with moments of discovery that remind everyone why they do this work. Without joy, theatre becomes mere work and drudgery, and audiences can sense it.

Shakespeare's plays require the company that performs them to be a united, hopeful and joyful team. Because the success of any Shakespearean production does not rest on a single actor, a single star, or even a single idea – it rests on the company, both on and off the stage.

If we believe in one another, if we support each other fully, if we are clearly having *fun* on stage, then the audience, too, will believe. And in that shared belief, Shakespeare's words will once again come alive.

But theatre-making is very difficult. There will be times when it looks like everything is falling apart, but the show must still go on.

This is when a company built on the principles of Unity, Hope and Joy will triumph through adversity – and one built on division, despair and misery will fail.

Top: The Exeter's Company including musicians, stage managers and dressers, gather onstage before the playhouse opens for A Midsummer Night's Dream at Pop-up Globe Perth, 2019. Bottom: The wider Pop-up Globe Theatre Company gathers for a photo at Pop-up Globe Auckland in late 2019. A company must be united, believe in the impossible, and find joy in their work.

The Queen's Company gather on-stage in the empty playhouse before the opening night of Much Ado About Nothing *at Pop-up Globe Auckland, 2017.*

Speaking Shakespeare

YOU WALK INTO THE rehearsal room on the first day. The air crackles with anticipation. Some faces are familiar, some famous, others unknown. Actors murmur lines to themselves, stretch, pace, size each other up. The weight of expectation is numbing. On the table, a stack of scripts. Shakespeare. The name alone carries its own gravity. And then the realization strikes: some of these people have lived inside these words longer than you have. They move with ease, fluent in the language of the verse. You wonder: *How do I even begin?*

Shakespeare never wrote a manual explaining his words. He left no guide, no footnotes, no 'correct' way to interpret them. And that means one thing: no one owns Shakespeare. Not the academics. Not the actors who have played Hamlet ten times over. Not the directors who spend their lives unpicking his text. His words belong to you.

The pulse of language

Whole books have been written about the rhythm of Shakespeare's language and how to approach it. Check out Patsy Rodenburg's books, or Kristin Linklater's. But to me, it's pretty straightforward. Shakespeare's language is alive. It moves, pulses, shifts. At its core is rhythm: iambic pentameter, that heartbeat of five da-DUMs per line. This is not a prison – it is a tool. It drives the thought, it carries the breath. It is the foundation of Shakespeare's world, the scaffolding upon which every speech is built.

In sooth, I know not why I am so sad... da-DUM da-DUM da-DUM da-DUM da-DUM.

Regular verse is steady, structured. But then – then the rhythm breaks. An extra beat sneaks in.

Here is one of the most famous lines in all of Shakespeare's work, Hamlet's legendary existential question.

To be or not to be, that is the quest-ion... da-DUM da-DUM da-DUM da-DUM da-DUM da.

That last syllable is weak, unfinished. A thought left open, unresolved. These irregularities are clues. A character's mind breaking, shifting, reforming. Thought and breath are intertwined – when the rhythm stumbles, so does the character's certainty.

Consider Macbeth after Duncan's murder. His verse fragments, his lines shorten, his rhythm falters. The iambic structure that once held him breaks apart just as his mind does. An actor who understands this inhabits the fracturing thoughts of a man undone by his own actions. When Macbeth says *Sleep no more*, the broken metre tells us as much about his state as the words themselves.

This is why you and your actors must scan every line of verse. Mechanically. Pencil in hand. Mark the stresses. Count the feet. Note the exceptions. This is not pedantry; it is the gateway to choice.

Is the stress in the normal place? Is it different? Why is it different? If you don't know, think laterally. Is the line short a syllable because there is a beat of silence, a pause, a piece of business that fills the gap? Or does the short line suggest something more fragile – a mind trailing off, a breath lost? Is the character jumbled, overflowing? Is this line even written in verse, or is it actually prose?

There is sometimes no definitive answer. Shakespeare left no handbook. And that is the point.

Your job is not to find the right answer. *Your job is to make choices.*

Bloody Good Shakespeare isn't about getting it 'right.' It's about getting it *alive*. The audience doesn't care about your scansion unless it leads to a more compelling performance. But they *do* feel it when something is real, when the actor is riding the wave of the verse, making choices that crackle with intention.

Making choices *is* the preparation. It's the hard, joyful work of rehearsal. The more bold choices you have made, the more alive the performance.

Remember that making Bloody Good Shakespeare means making Shakespeare that appeals to the full audience – ten-year-olds as well as the professors of Shakespeare. It's not enough to please one and not the other. The depth of preparation that comes from scanning verse closely and making thousands of choices is a critical part of your work in and around rehearsal. So do the work. Read the many excellent books about Shakespeare's verse and prose. Scan the lines. Dig into the verse. Hold workshops early in rehearsal to get everyone speaking the same language and thinking about the same problems. Build a shared vocabulary. Make the act of scanning and interpreting verse part of your company's culture.

The death of Shakespeare voice

The problem with Shakespeare, or rather the problem with the way Shakespeare is often performed, is that it too frequently dies on the tongue. The words, intended to pulse with life, instead calcify into something rigid, something preserved rather than experienced. And so, time and again, we find ourselves trapped in the echo chamber of 'Shakespeare voice,' that dreadful affectation where actors, in an effort to sound elevated, succeed only in sounding remote and artificial. We must begin, then, by dismantling this artifice, by rediscovering the naturalness that is always present in the text but too often buried beneath layers of reverence.

Shakespeare's language, spoken well, should feel as though it is being discovered in the moment, as though the actor is grasping for the next thought rather than reciting something polished and predetermined. The trick is to unearth the muscularity of the language, to find its rhythm without being enslaved by it, to allow thought and breath to shape the line rather than imposing an external sense of grandeur.

The first and simplest way to achieve this is to strip the text of any preconceptions. Do not think of it as poetry, even though much of Shakespeare's work operates in that heightened sphere. Instead, treat it as speech; urgent, necessary, something that must be thought as it is said. One of the greatest enemies of clarity is the tendency to luxuriate in the words, to stretch vowels, to lean into the language rather than letting it propel thought forward. But

Shakespeare did not write to be admired; he wrote to be understood. When performed well, his language will hit the audience with the vitality of real conversation.

There is no approved way to speak Shakespeare. There is no 'right' accent, or tone. There is only one thing: integrity. Use your own voice, revel in its unique power. Then if the role demands a specific accent, let this come out of your natural voice.

One note. Never, never amplify actors in live drama. The very idea is an affront to the form, regardless of the size of the theatre or its design. To place microphones on actors, to amplify their voices artificially, is to create distance between the actor and the audience. It has a deadly 'levelling' effect that makes everyone sound the same by narrowing the gate of volume and pitch, it undermines projection, and makes it difficult for the audience to follow who is speaking.

Worse, it leaves performances at the mercy of technical failure. Every theatre practitioner has heard or experienced the horror stories: an actor stepping off stage, forgetting to turn off their mic, and suddenly the entire audience is treated to the intimate details of their visit to the lavatory. More than a technical issue, it's an artistic failure. The human voice is theatre's most powerful instrument; nothing should come between it and the audience. Every actor must learn to command the space, to project to the back row, to make their voice carry with clarity and precision. This is the ancient art of theatre, something that cannot and should not be compromised by artificial amplification.

Beginning with meaning

The actor's job is first and foremost to communicate *meaning*. This is more important than anything else.

What is the character trying to say? What do they want? An actor must approach a monologue or a line as though they have no idea what they will say next. Too often, Shakespeare is spoken as if it is inevitable. But real speech is not inevitable. It is searching, questioning, responsive. Thought leads to thought, word to word. And so, the actor must let each idea unfold, must follow the text as though they are discovering it in real-time.

Take Juliet when she learns Romeo has killed Tybalt. Her thoughts race, contradict, evolve. She moves from shock to defence to doubt to resolution in the space of thirty lines. An actor who has predetermined how to speak these lines will miss the vital moment-to-moment discoveries that make the speech feel alive. Each thought must birth the next; each realisation must genuinely surprise.

One of the most powerful techniques to achieve this is to work physically. Shakespeare's language is built on action – on doing, not simply on speaking. If an actor finds themselves trapped in their head, trying to shape the perfect line reading, they are already lost. The body must be engaged. The breath must support the words. A line of verse is part of a physical event. This is why exercises that break up the rhythm – walking while speaking, changing direction on key thoughts, using the hands to emphasise shifts in argument – are invaluable. They remind the actor that the text is not something external but something lived.

Try this: Take a speech – Portia's *The quality of mercy is not strained* speech, perhaps, from *The Merchant of Venice* – and walk the space. Each time the thought shifts, change direction. When you reach a full stop, stop completely. When a question appears, physically reach out to someone. When you make a declaration, plant your feet. Soon, you'll find the body intuitively understands what the mind sometimes obscures – the physical shape of thought.

Verse and prose: the psychological map

And this is where verse and prose become particularly important. Too often, actors approach verse as something that must be treated differently from prose, as though the two are entirely separate species of speech. But the truth is that they exist on a continuum, and an actor must understand why Shakespeare switches between them.

Verse is structure. It is heightened thought, heightened emotion. It is the mind reaching for control, for eloquence. When a character speaks in verse, they are often trying to shape their world, to impose meaning upon chaos. But prose – prose is raw. It is the language of instinct, of ease, of release. When a character drops into prose, we see them stripped of artifice, speaking as their unguarded self.

Consider Hamlet. He is a prince, and so he speaks in verse. His mind is a labyrinth, and so his verse is complex, full of tangents and interruptions. But when he feigns madness, when he plays the fool, he slips into prose. The shift is not just linguistic – it is psychological. Verse is the voice of the prince; prose is the voice of the man trying to escape the weight of his own mind. And then, in moments of deepest introspection, when his thoughts are too tangled to unpick without more structure, he slips back into verse. This is where actors too often miss the truth of Shakespeare's language. The form reveals everything about a character's state of being.

And this is why the 'Shakespeare voice' must die. Because not only is it false, it flattens the text, rendering verse and prose alike into a uniform grandeur. But speech is not uniform. It is full of peaks and valleys, of shifts in tone and rhythm. When an actor allows themselves to be guided by this – when they let their breath, their thought, their impulse shape the line rather than the other way around – the result is something that does not 'sound like Shakespeare'. It sounds like life.

The breath of thought

Breath is critical. You do not breathe after you have thought. You breathe to think. When an actor truly understands this, the text becomes electric. A breath is not just a pause – it is an intention. Breathe at a full stop, at a colon, at a comma if the thought demands it. Breathe when you need to, not when you feel you should. Some actors are terrified of silence, of the moment between words. But Shakespeare lives in those spaces. A breath can be hesitation, discovery, or an impulse forming in real time.

Try this exercise: Take ten lines from any character. Now, perform the lines, breathing only where the punctuation indicates. Notice how this feels, how it shapes your understanding of the character's thought process. Now try it again, but breathe only when the thought changes, regardless of punctuation. These experiments reveal how breath shapes meaning, how the same words can convey entirely different mental states based solely on where you draw breath. This exposes the choices you must make in building a performance.

An actor cannot enter Shakespeare's world timidly. There is no room for hesitation. The heightened language – its metre, its muscularity – can be daunting, but within it lies a secret: the key to unlocking emotional truth is in the structure itself. I have always believed that when an actor truly listens to Shakespeare's rhythm, when they trust the breath of the line, they find themselves carried by it, rather than burdened by it. The iambic pentameter, so often treated as a cage, is in fact a current. Step into it, feel its pull, and suddenly, you are speaking from the core of the character's need, not from an intellectual effort to 'perform Shakespeare.' This process is one of surrender – to the text, to the breath, to the movement of thought that propels each speech forward.

Shakespeare must play you, not the other way around. If you force the lines, if you act upon them rather than letting them act upon you, something essential is lost. Consider that the actor must be a kind of lightly-tinted window through which we experience Shakespeare's text. The best actors understand that when they truly let the words inhabit them, they are simply conduits for something larger. And that is where magic happens.

There is an electricity within Shakespeare's language that cannot be tamed. His words are not meant to be spoken passively, not designed for the safety of polite recital. They demand to be lived. They demand breath, pulse, urgency. And yet, for so many actors, the challenge is not just in understanding the words, but in feeling them. In finding the immediacy that makes a speech necessary, rather than merely decorative. Shakespeare's language is alive with thought, and the actor's responsibility is to engage with that thought in real time, as if it were being spoken for the first time.

The chain of thinking

Long speeches are often where actors falter, where they retreat into performance rather than experience. The audience feels this immediately. A monologue or soliloquy that is spoken without discovery, without movement of thought, is a monologue that dies in the air. An actor must not simply know what they are saying; they must feel why they are saying it. Every line is an action, every phrase a shift. If there is no movement, no shift in energy, then the words, no matter how beautifully spoken, remain lifeless. Words without thought are sound and fury, signifying... nothing.

A great actor working with a monologue must become the communicator of a chain of thinking. A monologue is never simply words strung together

– it is always an argument, a case being made for a particular line of thought. The actor's job is to break it down into its constituent consecutive thoughts – each one a link in the chain. The greatest actors make sure that each link is clearly defined, each shift in thought distinctly marked. They take the audience with them on their journey of understanding. Without this clarity, even the most poetic speeches become impenetrable, and the audience is left adrift.

Take Shylock's *Hath not a Jew eyes?* speech. The argument progresses logically through a series of questions, assertions, and conclusions. An actor must make each step distinct, each new thought a discovery. When Shylock asks, *If you prick us, do we not bleed?*, it must feel like a genuine question, a thought occurring in that moment. The audience should watch the character think, reason, conclude. They should witness the birth of each new idea. Be clear, this isn't about 'over-thinking' the text. It's about showing the audience that *you are thinking as you speak*.

To do this, the actor must use every tool available to them: volume, pitch, pace, facial expression, physicality, stage movement, and direct address. A change in rhythm signals a change in thought. A shift in stance or a gesture can emphasise a revelation. A flicker in the eyes can suggest hesitation, self-doubt, or realisation. If these shifts are not clear, not planned, not thought through in detail during rehearsals, the argument of the monologue collapses, and the audience is left behind. But when an actor commits fully to communicating each step of the thought process, the monologue becomes alive with discovery, and the audience is taken on a journey of understanding. The words land, not as distant poetry, but as immediate truth.

Technical truth

There is a balance to be struck between technical accuracy and emotional authenticity. An actor too concerned with correctness will become rigid, confined by the 'rules' of verse. But an actor who disregards structure entirely will lose the very thing that makes Shakespeare sing. The answer lies in breath. Breath dictates thought, thought dictates feeling. The breath of the line, its natural ebb and flow, will always guide an actor to truth if they are willing to trust it. Breath is the bridge between the intellect and the body, the thing that turns words into living experience. When the actor allows breath to carry them, they stop speaking Shakespeare and start thinking Shakespeare.

In rehearsal, I tell actors to approach Shakespeare as they would a piece of music. No musician would play Beethoven without first feeling the rhythm in their body, without understanding the tension and release within a phrase. Shakespeare is the same. A speech must be played upon, tested, felt at different tempos, different intensities. I have seen performances transformed simply by changing the breath within a single line. A sudden intake before a crucial word, a held pause where before there was none – suddenly, meaning is illuminated. The power of Shakespeare's text is that it demands to be engaged with on multiple levels: intellectually, physically, emotionally. Rehearsal is the process of discovering how all these elements come together in performance.

For directors working with actors who struggle with the text, my advice is always this: take away the fear. The moment an actor feels they must be 'correct,' they will falter. Instead, break the text open. Let them move with it, whisper it, shout it, throw it away and find it again. Shakespeare's words are robust. They can take the weight of play, of exploration. And when an actor finally stops fighting the words and starts living in them, something remarkable happens. Their performance comes alive. Actors who enter the rehearsal room burdened by the weight of the text leave delighted when they discover that the text is not a barrier but a gateway. It is a living thing, and it waits only for the actor to breathe life into it and share it with the audience.

Only connect

We would never ask a student of Mozart to study his compositions without listening to them, yet we persist in treating Shakespeare as if his plays exist solely on the page. Peter Brook makes the analogy that Shakespeare's words are like lumps of coal. You can study them, weigh them, analyse their composition, but it is only when the coal is burned – *i.e.* the words are performed – that the energy is released and they fulfil their potential. Shakespeare's words are fuel for performance, meant to be ignited in the mouth of the actor.

The best performances are those that make the audience feel the immediacy of the language, as the characters are discovering their thoughts in real time. The actor's task is to ensure that the audience never falls behind, never loses the shared thread of thought. Each line is an argument made by the persuasive actor to the willing-to-be-persuaded audience.

So when you walk into a rehearsal room for the first time, let courage be your watchword. The courage to believe that you have as much right to Shakespeare as anyone else in the world. The courage to stand and speak as if the words were being discovered for the first time. The courage to trust that Shakespeare's text will carry you. The courage to live the language as a succession of spoken impulses rather than a performance. The courage to look the audience in the eye and connect.

And then something magical will take place: the gap between actor and audience will dissolve. We will share in the act of discovery. We will be present at the birth of thought. And in that moment, Shakespeare will be here, now, alive in the breath of the actor and the minds of the audience, united in the current of shared humanity across the centuries.

The Northumberland's Company led by Brigid Costello (left) rehearse a dance onstage for the final season of Pop-up Globe Auckland, 2019.

Top: The Southampton's Company perform a vocal and physical warmup on stage at Pop-up Globe Auckland, 2018. Bottom: Darcy Kent (Romeo) shows the physicality required in live action fight scenes in late-stage rehearsals for Romeo and Juliet at Pop-up Globe Auckland 2019-20.

Actor & Audience

WE'VE LOST OUR WAY. As film has grown exponentially, theatre has understandably become influenced by cinematic conventions. As directors increasingly work in cinema and actors and audiences grow up immersed in its grammar, many theatre-makers stage plays as though they are simply un-filmed movies.

I remember going to see a major touring production of an American play in London when I was in my twenties, staged in a proscenium-arch West End theatre with the audience facing the stage, in an 'end-on' configuration. The designers had masked the stage, leaving a 16:9 ratio gap through which the play unfolded, effectively creating a letterbox view. Every effort was made to present the play as film.

This approach is – like film itself – the ultimate expression of the 'fourth wall': a sealed-off world, presented as though real, that the audience observes but never influences. When the curtain rises, it reveals activity that has supposedly been happening all along. When it falls, we imagine the world of the play continuing in some way without us. In this way, the fourth wall gives the impression of a continuous, self-contained world that the audience glimpses only for a time, a 'slice of life'.

Realist theatre – 'kitchen sink' dramas, meticulously detailed settings, actors trained to maintain the illusion that no audience is present – depends on this wall. But the twentieth century brought theatre and film closer together, their methods and aesthetics converging. This has led to a shift in expectations, both from theatre-makers and audiences. A play staged in a hyper-realistic mode, with elaborate sets and cinematic lighting, risks prioritizing the language of cinema over theatrical presence.

Consider the fundamental differences between a theatre, where plays are staged, and a cinema, where films are screened. In a cinema, the audience sits in darkness, staring at a film on a fixed screen. The camera dictates what we see, and the illusion of realism is paramount. Laughter must be contained so as not to interrupt the film's set pacing. Audiences even police each other's behaviour, ensuring silence. In cinema, the film is a medium of control.

In contrast, universally-lit theatre encourages a two-way relationship between actors and spectators. In this theatre, the play is a medium of connection. The English stage has always been a creature of the crowd. Long before Shakespeare, medieval mystery cycles brought entire towns together to dramatise biblical stories in open streets and fields. These cycle plays – performed on pageant waggons by guild members – blended the sacred and the comic, the solemn and the bawdy. Devils and clowns cavorted alongside saints, and salvation came with a side of slapstick.

From this rowdy tradition emerged mummers' plays: rustic entertainments performed in inns and manor halls, especially at Christmas. They featured stock characters, ritual combat, and raucous humour. Saint George might slay the Turkish Knight, only for a comic Doctor to bumble in and bring him back to life. This was folk theatre as festive rite.

Shakespeare inherited this vernacular energy and transformed it. His plays are steeped in the DNA of English folk drama: cross-dressing, clowning, direct address, and festive inversion. His audiences, like those of the mystery plays, were not passive observers but vocal participants. Even in his darkest tragedies, there's room for truly comic characters. The stage was no sacred temple; it was a meeting place.

The very structure of those early playhouses, modeled on the galleried inns where early performances took place, insisted upon a dynamic interplay between actor and audience. Unlike the modern proscenium stage, which creates a firm separation between performers and viewers, these early theatres invited engagement. They were communal, proto-democratic spaces where story-making was a shared endeavor.

Elizabethan playhouses were vibrant social spaces. Theatregoing was not a hushed, reverent affair but a raucous, interactive event. Audiences did not merely watch; they responded. They cheered heroes and hissed villains. They laughed loudly at bawdy jokes and gasped at moments of high drama. They were drinking – weak ale was the staple beverage, safer than water in those days – and the energy in the yard must have been closer to that of a festival or a sporting event than a modern theatre with the audience sitting in polite silence. This kinetic energy influenced every aspect of performance, from the way actors projected their voices to the speed of delivery.

A culture of interaction has a profound effect on performance. Actors have to be alive to the crowd, responsive, ready to adapt. If an audience is particularly rowdy, they can lean into the chaos, use it, play off it. If an audience is attentive and serious, they can deepen into the stillness, drawing the crowd into their spell. Every performance is unique, shaped as much by the audience as by the actors. This interplay creates a thrilling theatrical experience, one that proscenium theatre, with its separation of performer and spectator, cannot really replicate.

Then came the rupture. In 1642, Puritan Parliament shut the theatres, branding them dens of vice. Public performance was banned, and actors pushed underground. But the folk instinct for theatre didn't die. Mummers kept playing in barns and back alleys. Jigs and comic turns lived on in fairs and farmhouses. Meanwhile, abroad, English performers absorbed Italian *commedia* and French spectacle – traditions of improvisation, masks, and physical transformation.

When Charles II returned in 1660, the theatres reopened with new flair: proscenium arches, painted scenery, and urbane wit. Out of this mix emerged eighteenth-century pantomime – a hybrid of *commedia's* Harlequinade, English Christmas misrule, and folk storytelling. Though pantomime doesn't trace a direct line from Shakespeare, it springs from the same deep well: a delight in play, spectacle, and shared laughter. And just like the Elizabethan stage, pantomime thrives on audience interaction. It revels in direct address, call and response, and the joyful dismantling of the fourth wall. The spirit of Shakespearean performance – the shared storytelling, the live exchange – lives on in the gleeful chaos of panto.

It's fashionable in some circles to sneer at pantomime, to dismiss it as lowbrow, trivial, or unsophisticated. This is snobbery, pure and simple – and a profound misunderstanding of the tradition. Panto is one of the few surviving forms of popular theatre that still demands the audience play along. In its riotous comedy, its joyous anarchy, and its brazen theatricality, it shares deep DNA with Shakespeare's stage. To turn up your nose at panto is to turn your back on the folk soul of English theatre itself.

Both pantomime and Shakespearean drama are born of the same instinct: theatre as a communal act. A place where the actor looks out and the audience looks back. Direct address collapses the wall between fiction and now, inviting complicity. Spectacle – a God descending from the heavens, a glittering transformation scene in a panto – is an invitation. A signal that here, together, something magical can happen.

In both forms, the audience is not a witness but a player. They're part of the game, the feast, the fiction. This interplay – visceral, electric – is what no screen or algorithm can replicate. The magic is not just in the story, but in the telling. Together.

And yet, even with all this exuberance, a myth persists. The myth of the hostile Elizabethan mob, hurling rotten fruit at actors they disliked. It's a persistent image – but a dubious one. While theatregoers were certainly vocal, even rowdy, the spirit of their engagement was playful, not contemptuous. As my fellow Pop-up Globe director Ben Naylor once remarked: throw something at an actor, and they're likely to throw it back. In universally lit productions, interaction arises in a spirit of complicity. It's a dance, not a duel.

Twelfth Night, Pop-up Globe Auckland, 2016. When a crisp packet fell onto the stage from a box above, Stephen Butterworth – playing Maria – didn't miss a beat. He picked it up, tasted a crisp, glanced at the audience with a 'meh' expression, then tossed it back to the audience member – who caught it. Cue applause. The play resumed. This seems to me to be in the true spirit that Shakespeare's theatre embraced.

By the time the Globe Theatre was built in 1599, playhouses had become sophisticated instruments of collective storytelling. The actor standing downstage centre was not merely performing; they were holding the centre of a communal ritual. Surrounded on all sides, visible to all, and seeing everyone in return, the actor became conjurer, storyteller, and catalyst. This is what makes the Elizabethan stage so potent – and why its spirit endures wherever theatre remembers it is a live, shared act.

Similarly, Pop-up Globe's spatial dynamic was immediately striking. The actor stood in the midst of 360 groundlings, with a further 500 audience members seated in galleries around and above. The audience was not just watching the play; they were part of the same world as the actor, breathing the same air, reacting in real time. There was no illusion of separation. No audience member was more than fifteen metres from the stage. Many of them were literally less than a metre away from the action. This environment reinforced Shakespeare's original vision: a theatre that pulsed with life, where the energy of the audience was just as critical as the words spoken onstage.

The lighting in these theatres was universal. The actors were not illuminated in isolation; the audience was equally visible, equally present. Their reactions, their energy, their laughter, or even their silence became part of the performance itself. A standing audience in the yard, packed tightly together, resembles a crowd at a public event or even a demonstration – volatile, engaged, even unruly. Shakespeare's plays were written for this charged atmosphere, where the boundary between fiction and reality is porous, where the play is a conversation rather than passively received.

The radical nature of direct address

On one level, we enter the theatre and surrender ourselves to the story, allowing events to unfold before us. This is 'that willing suspension of disbelief for the moment' described by Samuel Taylor Coleridge. Yet, at another level, we remain acutely aware that what we are witnessing is a performance – a crafted illusion brought to life by actors. We know it's not truly Hamlet standing before us but an actor playing the part. And the actor, too, knows we are there. This awareness, this mutual recognition between actor and audience, is where the magic of direct address begins.

When the audience is not merely present but *active*, their reactions – laughter, gasps, murmurs, silence – become part of the performance itself. In a space like the Globe, Shakespeare's soliloquies aren't private thoughts spoken aloud; they are conversations. They are a direct challenge, an invitation for the actor and audience to consider choices together. Soliloquies are moments of deep connection, where the audience isn't just watching – they're *participating*.

When I directed *Henry V* at Pop-up Globe in 2107, working with the brilliant Australian actor Chris Huntly-Turner and my long-term collaborator Assistant Director Eddie Bijl, we wanted to create the deepest possible connection between Chris as Henry V and the audience. We put our heads together and decided to underscore the Chorus's description of Henry V on the night before Agincourt by having Chris walk amongst the audiences in the yard, greeting his 'soldiers' in the form of individual audience members. They saw in real time what the Chorus described: *For forth he goes and visits all his host, / Bids them good morrow with a modest smile, / And calls them brothers, friends, and countrymen.*

Later, Henry returned to the yard to 'overhear' his cousin Westmoreland, up on the stage, fearfully wish for more soliders. From the midst of the audience Chris interjected, starting the famous *We happy few* soliloquy standing between his 'soldiers'. He stayed there for most of the speech, talking directly to his 'army', even embracing (respectfully, of course) audience members near him.

Similarly, the irrepressible actor Kieran Mortell created a powerful connection with the audience by acknowledging and involving them from the very beginning in his role as Dogberry in Miriama McDowell's 2017 *Much Ado About Nothing*. From involving them in playful songs and chants, to performing amongst the crowd in the yard and even the upper levels, Kieran embodied the connection between actor and audience to create the sense of shared storytelling and joyful unity that infused the entire production. At the end of this chapter are two images, one of Chris as Henry V and one of Kieran as Dogberry, making those physical connections with audience members that capture this idea perfectly.

This kind of interactive theatre – which we employed very widely across all of our productions – ensures that no two performances are ever the same. The mood of the audience, their responsiveness, even external factors like weather in an open-air space, all shape the experience. An actor skilled in direct address uses that shifting energy to guide their performance. It's a collaboration in real time.

If every audience brings a different energy, what anchors the meaning of a Shakespeare play? Is it what Shakespeare meant in 1601, say, or what tonight's audience takes away? The truth is that meaning is negotiated in the moment. Of course, the script provides structure, character, and plot. But when we stage Shakespeare with open light and no fourth wall, we invite the audience to become co-creators. Their presence changes the stakes.

Yes, the play ends the same way. Romeo still dies. Henry still wins. But when a crowd cheers for Henry V before Agincourt, they're not trying to rewrite the ending – they're *participating* in its triumph. Like supporters at a football match, their cheers don't directly change the score – but they change the *feeling* of the game. In theatre, that feeling is everything. It's what makes a scripted moment feel *alive*.

I've seen this first-hand. In Melbourne, the yard went wild for *Henry V*. Even though Australians aren't exactly known for their enthusiasm for the English monarchy, there I was – surrounded by sunburned, happy Aussies chanting *England! England!* as though their lives depended on it. They *wanted* to be part of Henry's army. They *chose* to cheer, to chant, to ride into battle with him. On that blistering 39-degree day, I felt closer to the English army of 1415 than I ever have, because it was *happening around me*.

In this context, direct address and universal lighting are radical acts. They shatter the illusion of separation. They demand something different from the actor, the audience, and the play. This is anti-realist theatre.

As an audience member, I have always enjoyed being acknowledged. It makes me feel like I am getting my money's worth. Otherwise, watching theatre can feel like paying to worship at the altar of the actor's ego. It's totally clear to me now that one of the defining features of Shakespeare's theatre is direct address: actors speaking directly to the audience, making eye contact, drawing them into the world of the play. In Bloody Good Shakespeare, the audience must be not only acknowledged but actively incorporated into the storytelling.

Direct Address as cultural reconnection

We live in an age where attention is fractured and presence is rare. Young people, in particular, are spending more time alone, more time online, and more time in digital spaces where human connection is mediated by screens. Post-pandemic, the very idea of gathering together in a physical space – especially one where we might be seen, might be asked to engage – can provoke anxiety rather than excitement.

This is where Shakespeare can help.

In the shared light of a space like the Pop-up Globe, direct address is a radical invitation to return to community. It breaks the fourth wall not just theatrically, but socially. It offers an alternative to the curated performances of social media and the isolating algorithms of doomscrolling. Instead, it says: you are here, you matter, and this story *needs you*.

When an actor looks a teenager in the eye and asks – *To be, or not to be?* – it's no longer a rhetorical question. It's a real one. That young person becomes implicated, responsible, alive in the moment. Theatre becomes a rehearsal for real life. It trains us in empathy, in listening, in response. It draws us out of our bedrooms and into the *agora*, the public square.

And perhaps, in doing so, it helps repair the fabric of a society frayed by disconnection.

This is what makes direct address not just powerful, but necessary and socially important. In a world that increasingly encourages passivity, distraction, and isolation, direct address demands that we look up, put down the phone, and engage. And in that cathartic engagement, we will start to find not just the meaning of the play, but the meaning of ourselves.

Practical approaches to direct address

To revitalize Shakespeare, you must embrace the power of direct address. You must train your actors to look at the audience directly in their eyes, to speak to them as if they were confidants, co-conspirators, or fellow players in the drama. The effect is remarkable. Audiences won't merely watch; they will participate.

But for actors unused to direct address, building confidence in engaging with the audience can take time.

At Pop-up Globe, we trained actors in a technique to keep audience engagement fluid and dynamic. We called it 'passing the baton.'

The principle was simple: an actor receives a line from their scene partner, starts to respond directly to them, then picks up the energy to direct the central part of their line outward to the audience before bringing the final few words back to their partner, passing the baton of focus and energy. It's a bit like watching a game of tennis, with the energy of focus passed backwards and forwards between the actors on stage and the audience.

This exercise helped actors break free from the misconception that direct address is a binary choice. The audience is always included in the energy of the performance, but not every moment must be played solely to them. The trick is knowing when and how to extend and retract that energy. Actors who master this technique ensure that the audience remains engaged in the story rather than merely observing it from a distance.

A particularly effective technique is gestural redirection. The actor points to one place but directs their spoken words elsewhere. This allows for a physical connection – perhaps gesturing to heaven or hell while speaking to the audience, or vice versa – without losing engagement with the scene's intended focus. Such techniques allow for multiple levels of engagement, keeping performances dynamic and multifaceted.

Here are some more exercises designed to strengthen that connection:

The eye contact challenge

Have an actor perform a soliloquy while making direct eye contact with individual audience members (or fellow actors acting as stand-ins).

Instead of scanning the crowd vaguely, they should pick specific people and speak to them directly, allowing real interaction to shape their delivery. The actor should deliver only one thought to each audience member, before moving on to the next. Do not dwell too long with one individual, keep the direction fluid.

This exercise fosters awareness and helps the actor gauge and adjust their performance based on the audience's reaction.

Call and response

In groups, actors take turns delivering Shakespearean lines that invite an audience response (*e.g. Hath not a Jew eyes?*). The 'audience' responds however they see fit – laughing, booing, cheering – and the actor must adjust their performance accordingly. This builds responsiveness and confidence in live interaction.

For directors looking to harness this superpower, here are some essential techniques that must be used throughout the rehearsal process, from the very beginning:

Encourage eye contact

Actors must connect with individual audience members, or frankly anyone off-stage in the rehearsal room, using direct address to engage them in the storytelling. It's critical to flex this muscle as most modern actors, trained for film and television, initially find this fairly unnatural and initially distracting or off-putting. Persevere!

In my experience the actors who initially resist often become the greatest champions for direct address once they understand how it enlivens their performance and helps them connect.

Use the whole stage

Movement must be bold and intentional. Remember that the audience surrounds the actor, and the performance must effectively play in 360 degrees. Use the whole stage to keep the scene in motion, using new thoughts and impulses in the text to initiate stage movement.

Emphasise vocal energy

Without the aid of microphones, projection and clarity are vital. The voice must reach the furthest corners of the theatre. The vocal health of actors is critical – engage the services of a voice coach to give actors the tools they need to maintain and enhance their vocal energy.

Invite audience response

Whether through laughter, murmurs, or gasps, audience reaction must be sought, acknowledged and incorporated, validated or questioned, accepted or even rejected.

Rehearse with the audience in mind

Instead of treating rehearsals as closed processes, bring in test audiences early to see what works. Anyone will do to begin with – stage managers, other actors.

Direct address must be purposeful, not random. Determine how moments benefit from audience engagement and shape performances accordingly.

A case study: *Much Ado About Nothing*

Let's look at this in action, at the start of the wedding scene from *Much Ado About Nothing*, 4.i, where Claudio humiliates Hero before their assembled friends and family. It's a scene built for direct address.

Direct address works when the audience takes on a role within the scene. In a wedding, this is obvious: they become wedding guests. This principle applies to most of Shakespeare's scenes: courtroom scenes, public speeches, even intimate moments where the audience can be imagined as confidants.

The key distinction is between public and private moments. In a wedding, some exchanges are public, meant for all to hear, while others are intended to be 'private', that is to say, meant for other on-stage characters to hear. Let's be clear at once that everything spoken on a stage must be clearly audible to the audience. But private lines can be played 'inwards' upon the stage. Public lines must be played 'outwards', to the audience. It is a question of intent and focus, not sound levels.

Leonato begins the scene privately, speaking only to the Friar:

Come, Friar Francis, be brief; only to the plain form of marriage, and you shall recount their particular duties afterwards.

This is a practical note to the officiant, essentially, *let's keep this short*. It's an aside within the public event. Then the Friar speaks, addressing Claudio in a fully public statement:

You come hither, my lord, to marry this lady?

This is the moment where the marriage is meant to proceed smoothly. But Claudio responds not with an expected *Yes*, but with *No*.

A stunned silence follows. The audience, positioned as wedding guests, must process the shock in real-time. Leonato attempts to publicly smooth things over, assuming Claudio has misunderstood the question:

To be married <u>to her</u>, Friar. You come to marry her.

Perhaps there's a ripple of laughter, an awkward attempt to cover the misstep. But when the Friar turns to Hero and asks, *Lady, you come hither to be married to this count?* and she answers publicly, *I do*, the moment of dramatic tension stretches even further. Then comes the friar's fateful public line:

If either of you know any inward impediment why you should not be conjoined, I charge you on your souls to utter it.

This phrase is echoed in countless wedding ceremonies, both in fiction and reality, and it serves as a kind of dramatic ticking clock. Will someone object? And of course, someone does. I would ask the actors on stage to turn to the crowd, to look for any objections. There will almost certainly be none from the audience. So when one does come, from the stage, it feels even more shocking.

Claudio makes his accusation publicly, shattering the moment and launching the scene into chaos. The audience, as wedding guests, are suddenly embroiled in scandal. Do they side with Claudio? With Hero? Do they gasp? Do they shift uncomfortably? The audience's visible and vocal reactions shape the play in real-time.

When we cast the audience in a role – be it as witnesses, confidants, or members of a crowd – the scene transforms. Here, it shifts into something akin to a Jerry Springer showdown. The groom makes outlandish accusations, the bride's supporters leap to her defense, and the groom's allies rally behind him. But crucially, each side is also appealing to the audience for support. The audience becomes part of the scene's energy, and the stakes are raised immeasurably. This sense of active participation heightens the drama, drawing the audience into the emotional core of the play rather than leaving them as passive onlookers.

Shakespeare embeds signals in his text for when actors should engage the audience. Some of these are explicit: soliloquies, plural pronouns, or direct questions. Others are more subtle but equally powerful:

- **Plural usage**: If a character addresses 'you' in the plural, why not play to the widest possible 'you' – the audience? In *Twelfth Night*, Malvolio's final line, *I'll be revenged on the whole pack of you*, gains power when delivered to the entire theatre. The audience becomes complicit. Are we the pack? Is his revenge on us too? The direct address in such moments turns theatre into something more akin to a political rally or a courtroom, where the audience's reaction and participation are part of the event.

- **Scenes in public places**: Any time a scene is set in a town square, a battlefield, or a court, we must ask: who is witnessing this? If the scene involves persuasion or rhetoric, the audience is a natural recipient of the argument.

- **Decision moments**: If a character must make a decision, let them visually 'check in' with the audience – and make the decision with them, before informing other on-stage characters of their choice.

- **Casting audience as off-stage characters**: When Nerrissa describes Portia's suitors in *The Merchant of Venice*, it's a perfect opportunity to cast individual audience members as the suitors, and for Nerrisa and Portia to consider – and reject them – in real time.

- **Plays within plays**: When a performance happens inside a performance, it throws a spotlight on the act of theatre itself, breaking down barriers between actor and audience. *A Midsummer Night's Dream* offers one of the finest examples with the Mechanicals' absurdly earnest *Pyramus and Thisbe*. At Pop-up Globe, we seized this opportunity to deepen audience interaction. We set the Mechanicals' play downstage, where they could shamelessly perform to the yard. Upstage, the nobles sat adjacent to real audience members in the Lords' Rooms, offering live commentary – jeering, laughing, and interrupting. This layered the performance, pulling the audience into the action. At first, they laughed with the nobles. But as the aristocrats' mockery grew cruel, the audience's sympathy shifted to the Mechanicals. They began cheering for Bottom and his company, even shouting down the nobles' dismissive taunts. To heighten the fun, we staged Pyramus and Thisbe's deaths as ridiculously bloody. When Thisbe prepared to stab herself, she wickedly threatened the audience with the stage blood they knew would be coming. They recoiled, shrieking and laughing in equal measure – before she finally plunged the blade in, sending a spectacular arc of blood onto the groundlings.

A director's starting point should be that almost all of Shakespeare is designed for direct address. These textual signals are opportunities to go even further.

Common pitfalls in direct address

Newcomers to direct address often fall into the same traps. The first mistake is not knowing their lines well enough. Direct address increases an actor's vulnerability, and if they are at all shaky on the text, eye contact with an audience will derail them.

Actors! Know your lines so well that they are no longer lines. They are your thoughts. They must live in you, sit in your bones. You must be able to say them while running, while laughing, while looking a stranger dead in the eye. If you don't know them at that level, you are not ready. Because the moment you step on stage and lock eyes with an audience member, something happens. If you are not fully prepared, that moment will steal your line. The eye contact will strip your mind blank. The audience is there, in real time, and suddenly you are exposed. If you don't know your lines utterly, you will panic. But if you do know them – if they are second nature – then eye contact will not take from you. It will give. It will feed your performance, make the words now, make them true.

Another frequent issue is failing to return the energy to the stage. An actor who engages 'outward' to the audience but does not refocus the energy 'inward' to the stage leaves the scene hanging, like an unresolved conversation. The audience must feel part of the exchange, but the actor must always bring the moment back into the play's world and pass the baton of energy onto a scene partner. Otherwise, we risk dropping momentum and splitting audience focus. The audience will look where the actor looks. If the actor continues to hold the audience's eyes, the energy is interrupted and the actor's scene partner is left with nothing.

Then there's the misuse of direct address: belittling or intimidating audience members, holding eye contact too long, or failing to vary engagement. An actor should never make an audience member feel trapped. Keep moving. Deliver a single line, half a line, even a word or a gesture to one person, then slide away. Variety keeps the energy alive. The key is to ensure that the audience's role as participants enhances their enjoyment rather than making them feel uncomfortable.

The false separation of actor and audience

The biggest question that comes up with direct address is: *How do you balance engaging the audience while staying in the world of the play?* To me, this question assumes a false separation. In direct address theatre, particularly in universal lighting conditions, there is no distinct 'world of the play' separate from the world of the audience. There is only the shared moment of story-telling.

When Shakespeare's actors stepped onto the stage at the original Globe, they didn't leave the real world behind; they stepped into an amplified version of it. Their world and the audience's world were one and the same. That remains true today. The sooner actors embrace that unity, the more powerful their performances will become. Theatres that employ universal lighting conditions naturally facilitate this connection, dissolving the boundary between actor and audience.

In Shakespeare, the audience isn't just watching the play, they are part of it. They are Hamlet's conscience, Richard III's co-conspirators, and Sir Toby Belch's drinking companions. To exclude them is to flatten the experience into something far less immediate, less dangerous, and less true to the spirit of the work.

This is what we rediscovered at Pop-up Globe. That is why direct address is not a trick, but a necessity. That is why Shakespeare, when staged this way, feels not like the past but like the present, happening now, with all the urgency, humor, and danger he intended. To see a character confide in you, to be drawn into their schemes or sympathies, is to feel the play is happening with you, not just in front of you. It transforms Shakespeare's works from historical artifacts into something present and deeply felt. This is why theatre, when it is true to its own form, is unparalleled in its transformative impact on audiences.

So, the next time you direct or perform Shakespeare, don't ask yourself whether you should address the audience. Ask yourself instead – why wouldn't you? The audience is your most valuable scene partner, and their presence is not a challenge to overcome but a gift to embrace.

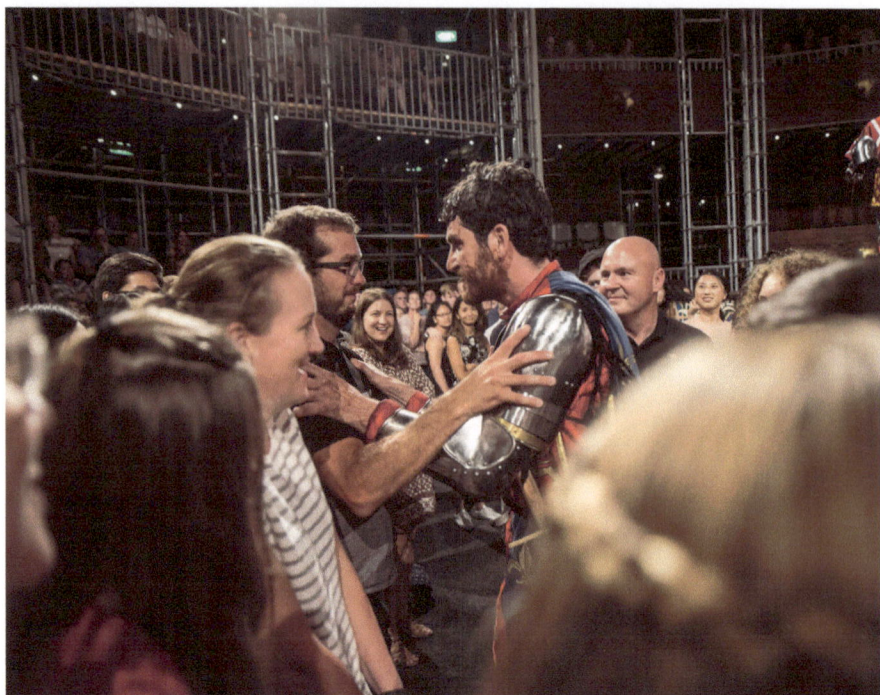

Making physical contact with the audience creates communal storytelling. Top: Henry V (Chris Huntly-Turner) embraces an audience member during the 'We happy few' soliloquy on the morning of Agincourt during Henry V at Pop-up Globe Auckland, 2017. Bottom: Dogberry (Kieran Mortell) shakes hands from the stage during Much Ado About Nothing at Pop-up Globe Auckland, 2017.

Top: Young audience members are drawn deeply into the emotion of Romeo & Juliet at Pop-up Globe Auckland, 2020. Many young people became 'super fans', attending multiple performances, often in home-made costumes. Below: Audience members cheer the cast of Much Ado About Nothing at Pop-up Globe Melbourne, 2017.

Top: Bottom (Mike Edwards), transformed into a terrifying Ass, chases the 'tradie' mechanicals at Pop-up Globe Aauckland, 2017. Bottom: Puck (Jade Daniels) in A Midsummer Night's Dream at Pop-up Globe Sydney, 2018.

Rehearsing Shakespeare

REHEARSING SHAKESPEARE BEGINS LONG before the actors step into the rehearsal room. By the time rehearsals commence, key decisions have already been made: the play, the setting, the costumes (at least in design if not yet in fabric), the cast, and the performance space. These elements shape the production's look and feel, its energy, its approach, its possibilities – and its limits. They form the container in which your work will unfold.

The moment before rehearsal begins can be terrifying. For the director. For the actors. The empty space waits. This is the precipice from which all great theatre leaps. There is no safety net. But there is also no excuse for the director who arrives unprepared. You must come armed. Armed with understanding, with intention, with a readiness to lead not from ego, but from clarity and care.

By the time actors and director step into that charged space, the initial textual work and thinking must already be done. You must know the world of the play. You must understand every word you – or your actors – will speak. Know the lines inside out. You don't need to be a Shakespearean scholar, but you must be a fearless explorer of the text.

The director's first job is not to impose a vision – it is to form a team. To put people at ease. You are not on trial. You are the servant leader. Whatever energy you bring to that room will echo across weeks of work. Set the tone with confidence, curiosity, and care. Instill unity. Offer hope. Encourage joy.

And remember this: rehearsing Shakespeare is not the same as rehearsing a modern play. While some principles are universal – come prepared, build ensemble, create space for play – the Shakespearean director must wield a different toolkit.

In Shakespeare, the language is not just the script. It is the set, the lighting, the action. Every emotion, every beat of staging is embedded in the spoken text. To direct Shakespeare is to orchestrate rhythm, thought, breath, and rhetoric. It is to unlock character through sound and structure.

Unlike modern playwrights – think of Tom Stoppard, for example – Shakespeare gives you almost no stage directions. Apart from entrances and exits (and the occasional *Dies* or *Sleeps*, or *Exit, pursued by a bear*), everything else must be interpreted from the text itself. There are no helpful notes about tone, pace, or blocking. The clues are all in the rhythm, the imagery, the shifts in metre and thought. This demands a far greater level of textual analysis from the director and actors alike. In a Stoppard script, a pause might be indicated and a moment carefully prescribed. In Shakespeare, the pause is felt, not written. You must find it through breath, syntax, and structure.

The audience relationship is different, too. The actor sees the audience – and the audience sees the actor. The energy flows both ways.

This is ritual, not realism. Mythic, not naturalistic. And that changes everything.

Can a non-Shakespeare director make the leap? Absolutely. But you must leave behind certain habits. You must shift from subtext to structure. From naturalism to heightened reality. From concept to craft. If you can do that – and if you come ready to play – you'll find that Shakespeare gives back tenfold. Whatever energy you bring to that room will set the tone for a long time to come. This chapter is to give you some tools to help you on that road. Remember – instilling a sense of unity, hope and joy is at the heart of the director's job. You don't need to be a world-expert in Shakespeare, just ready to play with the actors to make the production *together*.

Many years ago I had an experience working with an amateur company – as an actor. It was eye-opening. What struck me most was that rehearsals were extremely serious, with little playfulness. Then, in performance, the atmosphere backstage was a riot of laughter, pranks, and chaos. In professional theatre, it is exactly the opposite: rehearsals are full of laughter and play, while performances are taken very seriously. That contrast is key to understanding the professional approach to theatre. Play in rehearsal fosters creativity and allows actors to take risks, while precision in performance ensures consistency and impact. This balance of seriousness and playfulness, discipline and freedom, is the hallmark of truly professional work.

Instill a rhythm to each day of rehearsal. At Pop-up Globe, we began each rehearsal with a karakia, a Māori form of prayer, then a discussion about the plan ahead, and we ended the day with another group discussion and a karakia to close. Standing in a circle, giving every actor a chance to speak about the day. These sessions were an opportunity for people to thank each other, voice concerns, or simply reflect. Often, discussions became quite robust. It's crucial to give actors the space to express themselves, maintaining an environment where they feel heard and valued. An ensemble that communicates openly will always create richer, more meaningful work on stage. These rituals create a container for the work, sanctifying the space and the time spent within it.

The length of rehearsal time varies dramatically. The most extreme example in my early career was staging three productions simultaneously in seventeen days, with a cast working in repertory. It was a baptism of fire. Actors arrived knowing their lines, and our primary goal was to get the plays up on their feet as fast as possible. That's not an approach I'd recommend for Shakespeare, but necessity dictated it at the time. Pop-up Globe rehearsed for six weeks, working on two productions at once. This is just enough time to discover the heat at the heart of the play.

A director must complete their textual work thoroughly before day one. Understanding each line, each image, each reference provides the foundation upon which everything else is built. This doesn't mean having every moment pre-staged, but rather having such intimate knowledge of the text that you can respond with instinctive confidence to whatever emerges in rehearsal. You must hold the map of the play in your mind, while allowing the journey to unfold with the actors.

The first days: forging the fellowship

The first day of rehearsals is not about Shakespeare. It is about human beings entering a room together, preparing to make something extraordinary. Two things must be achieved.

First, an understanding of the conditions of performance, including direct address and the relationship to the audience. This is easily achieved through a workshop session that explores these practices and ensures a shared understanding that will evolve through rehearsals. Shakespeare demands connection; his words are alive when they are spoken directly to someone. Without this fundamental interaction, performances risk feeling distant and unengaging. So it's absolutely critical that direct address is part of the way of working from the very beginning. It's not something you can add in later on, like frosting on a cake. I encourage actors to maintain eye contact with the audience, even if I am the only audience in the room. Actors should practice delivering their lines 'outwards' even if there's no one there, to try to bake in the idea of delivery 'outside' the stage area. The audience is not an observer but a participant in the drama, and actors must learn to embrace this relationship from the start.

Second, and more vital: this is the day that the fellowship of the company begins. The company must coalesce before the work can flourish. One of the best ways to do this is through a collective challenge unrelated to the play itself, something physical, engaging, and preferably a little ridiculous. I've had companies build sandcastles together, crowd into a pub, even clean graffiti off a nearby wall. At Pop-up Globe, we would take our actors to see the theatre under construction, to let them walk the space before a single word had been spoken in it. Their footsteps echoed on the wooden floors, their voices testing the acoustics, their hands touching the bare metal of the scaffolding. They began to sense the space as theirs before the audience would claim it. Anything that bonds the group in a shared experience works.

The first day is not the time for the director to talk too much, to be severe or overly intense. The role of the director is to lead, but also to listen. Establish a light, open atmosphere. Ensure that every single person there is given an opportunity to speak, to show a little of who they are. If the team leaves that first day feeling unified, hopeful and having fun, you've laid a foundation for good work to come.

On the second day, the real work begins. Many directors feel the first thing to do is sit down and read the play aloud together, the so-called table read. I did this for years, despite finding it an uninspiring exercise. Most actors, understandably, don't want to act fully in a first read. There's too much unknown. So what results is often a flat, mumbling, half-hearted experience that benefits no one. As a friend once observed, when you slump around for a table read, the text slumps around with you. Yet, because I couldn't think of an alternative, I persisted with it.

Then after many years I decided I simply couldn't bear doing these read-throughs anymore, and I decided to dispense with the table read all together. Instead, I decided to start rehearsing without one. That saved about five hours of rehearsal time for the full company, but it also had its drawbacks. Sometimes actors who hadn't done the necessary preparation were caught off guard by action they hadn't anticipated or didn't realise they were in certain scenes. So we had to replace the read-through with something else, something more alive, more immediate.

Where I eventually landed is to stumble through the entire play on the afternoon of the second day, once we've all met and been through group workshops on direct address and approaches to verse. Instead of sitting around reading, put the play on its feet immediately. Hand in hand with this, I insist that all actors have learned their lines before rehearsals commence. There's no real way to act with a script in your hand. That's reading, not acting. This insistence on arriving off-script helps everyone immensely.

In this initial stumble, actors are welcome to use their scripts for reference or notes if they wish, and there's a helpful and non-judgemental prompter available at all times. Mark out an approximate stage space and establish a simple movement rule: all entrances from stage right upstage, all exits to stage left upstage. If an actor has to re-enter the scene, they do so from stage left upstage again. This approach won't work for every scene, of course, but it is enough to reveal the overall shape of the play. You will begin to understand the rhythm of scenes, their relative length, and most importantly, you will all find it far more engaging to watch actors moving and interacting than listening to them drone through a script.

Insist on an active approach to moments that obviously require movement. If the text calls for a fight, improvise a safe 'playing' version of the fight straight away. If there is a song, and you have the music, everyone sings it, not just the designated actor. If a prop is needed, encourage actors to use a placeholder, which will prove immensely useful for the creative team.

The fight director, the stage manager, the music director, and the movement coach will all gain immediate insight into how the actors move, how they use the space, and how certain elements might be incorporated, cut or changed. The director can make immediate notes about staging choices, and you can start planning ensemble involvement right away. It highlights which actors might need additional support, where transitions might be tricky, and how you can shape the ensemble.

If everyone knows from the beginning which scenes they are in as named characters, and the ones in which they'll be in the ensemble, they start to see their part in the larger theatrical dance, the way their character moves through the world of the play and the production. The energy in the room will be palpable – not the famously dead air of a read-through, but the living breath of theatre taking shape.

Best of all, this gives the director a crucial piece of information: the likely run time. This must be kept as tight as possible. Shakespeare's plays, left unchecked, can sprawl. But strict rules around length must apply if you want your audience to enjoy their evening. A production that outstays its welcome loses its grip; its inevitability becomes drudgery.

Shakespeare gives it to us directly in *Romeo and Juliet*: the two hours' traffic of our stage. Two hours. Maybe slightly longer. It seems unlikely given the density of his text, but we must assume that Elizabethan and Jacobean performances rarely exceeded three hours. Likely, they aimed closer to two, running straight through with no interval.

And yet, look at *Hamlet*. A full folio text runs over four hours if spoken in its entirety. Did Shakespeare's actors really perform every word? Unlikely. When we examine the so-called 'bad quartos' – those early printed versions of the plays, often much shorter versions than given in the folio or in modern conflated texts – it becomes clear that variation was built into the process. Different versions of a play existed for different circumstances. Just as modern companies shape productions to fit a venue, an audience, a company of actors, so too must Shakespeare's company have cut, adapted, and streamlined these longer versions.

At Pop-up Globe, we agreed a strict rule: no production could run longer than two hours and fifteen minutes. The first half could be no more than seventy-five minutes. What we found was that this forced a kind of discipline, a precision in storytelling. It stripped away indulgence, leaving only the necessary. And that necessity – that raw, distilled energy – is what made the plays sing.

If a production must run straight through without an interval, then it must be cut to under two hours, preferably ninety minutes. The pace must be relentless, the production ever-expanding.

There is another important reason for a tight run time, a strictly practical one. Every minute of stage action has what might be called a 'technical debt'. This debt is the time spent rehearsing that minute. In a tight full-time three-week rehearsal process for a single show, that's about eighty minutes of rehearsal time for every on-stage minute. You can see why checking the run time early and then editing the script down accordingly is so useful in order to make the tightest, best-rehearsed show possible.

In a busy company with days where there are two, or even three, shows scheduled, the run time is of course paramount. There must be time for resetting the production, and for the company to take breaks. Unexpectedly long run times result in really serious – and sometimes expensive – problems for the cast, crew and management.

Consider very carefully the space in which you rehearse. It is always a good idea, when possible, to rehearse outdoors. Rehearsal rooms lie to you. They are a false friend. Indoors in smaller spaces, voices feel fuller, sound bounces back, and you can be lulled into thinking projection is sufficient. But outdoors is more truthful. When you rehearse outside, you quickly learn how much effort is needed to be heard and how distractions (wind, birds, passersby) force you to sharpen your focus. The open air demands bigger gestural performance, more grounded vocal projection, much clearer storytelling, and more present engagement with your fellow actors.

Strengthening the actor's voice is a huge advantage of this practice, ensuring they develop the stamina needed to sustain performances. At Pop-up Globe, we would often take scenes into the gardens behind our rehearsal space, letting the elements challenge and shape the work, bringing a robust focus to the performances that served us well in the large playhouse.

The power of the ensemble

Understanding and using the ensemble is something a Shakespeare director must consider from the outset. The ensemble is the invisible engine of great theatre. It brings depth, texture, and dynamism to the world of the play.

We start with the *Company* – everyone who makes the production happen, from actors to dressers to directors. Within that, the *Acting Company* – the performers themselves, each with their individual *roles*. (I was fascinated to learn many years ago that the term 'roles' is drawn literally from the playing scripts handed out, each containing only that actor's part of the script, rolled up over two pieces of wood so it could be scrolled through for easy reference. *Here is your roll/role.*) But beyond these named parts lies something just as vital: the *ensemble*.

The ensemble consists of actors present in multiple scenes, often doubling when they are not required in their principal roles. They are the sailors, the monks, the townspeople, the soldiers – the figures who populate Shakespeare's worlds, making them feel alive. They used to be called 'spear carriers,' but that term diminishes their importance. A great ensemble can shift tone in an instant – laughter one moment, menace the next. They create scale, making a court feel grand, a battlefield feel chaotic, a city feel bustling. Done well, the ensemble is a storytelling force in its own right, shaping scenes not just as background but as an active, reactive presence. They are the breath of the world, the tide that turns the play.

Pop-up Globe's *Henry V* was the first time I used an ensemble properly. The play's legendary battle scenes were staged with only fifteen actors and two musicians. While that may sound like a reasonable number, when staging a battle like Agincourt, it quickly feels insufficient – two armies of seven actors each? Not ideal. The ensemble was so vital to the production that every actor, apart from Henry himself, was part of it. We roped in 'acting' stage managers, musicians, every available body, all in disguise to bulk out the ensemble. It was immense fun, and led to extraordinarily fun and frenetic stage business.

The intense onstage action was mirrored by equally intense offstage work. Quick costume changes – so complex they required a backstage team of five – meant actors barely had a moment to rest. Mud and blood were applied and wiped off in seconds, while off-stage sound effects, from battle noises to songs, added to the chaos. The backstage area became a whirlwind of flying costumes, sweating actors, and hasty transformations. No member of the company was ever still.

If audiences could have seen both sides of the production, the onstage drama and the offstage chaos, they would have witnessed an astonishing feat of theatrical athleticism. That energy fed directly into the performances, giving them an urgency and vitality that transcended the limitations of our numbers. The mirror between off-stage and on-stage action was staggering in its power and potential.

To use your ensemble effectively, you must create a scene plot that details not only which actors are required as named characters in each scene but also highlights who is *not* required. This second list is invaluable. If you know which actors are free during a scene, you can bring them on as ensemble members. Most actors enjoy as much stage time as possible, and finding ways to involve them beyond their primary roles enhances the overall theatrical experience. It turns the play into a living, breathing world rather than a series of isolated exchanges. And it's a lot of fun.

This is the kind of creative problem-solving that ensemble use allows. In *Twelfth Night*, we had a group of anonymous sailors in striped tops and false moustaches – anyone could be a sailor, making doubling easy. In our Sydney season of *Macbeth*, we created an ensemble of ominous hooded monks, their faces shrouded in shadow, adding tension and a warped spirituality to a world of witches and demons. When Banquo's ghost appeared at the feast, these monks slowly turned their hooded faces toward Macbeth, becoming part of his nightmarish vision. In *The Comedy of Errors*, they were townspeople and bearded 'whirling dervish' accomplices of Dr. Pinch, creating the illusion of a bustling city. At the end of the play, they formed a comic mob pursuing the leads around the stage – a deeply satisfying and hilarious climax that grew organically from their presence throughout. Note that your ensemble's disguises must be effective at transforming your actors, otherwise you risk confusing your audience.

The ensemble is the director's secret weapon. Strong ensembles bring Shakespeare's worlds to life, and that process begins on the first day of rehearsals.

Staging approaches: finding the shape

Blocking must emerge from the play itself. Some directors apparently arrive at rehearsals with a fully mapped-out vision of where every actor should stand in every moment. I would find this stifling and dictatorial, and I'm sure the actors would too. By all means start blocking by giving your actors a place to enter from. But from there, work with your actors to find the shape of a scene through structured play with low stakes. Make sure the company understands that 'one must start somewhere', that work made on the first take of a scene is entirely disposable and will evolve into something entirely different and more impressive through the rehearsal process. Run a scene multiple ways, playing with proximity and separation. Through this, the actors start to feel the natural gravitational forces of the play, and blocking will emerge organically, like water finding its course down a hillside.

It's the directors role to balance this organic blocking with the needs of the audience and the strengths of the given stage. A thrust stage can be imagined as looking like the side of a die that shows the number five, with four strong positions in the corners and one central pivot point. The centre and down-stage centre of the stage is always a place of power, and major confrontations should take advantage of this focal point, drawing the audience's eye to the heart of the dramatic tension. All stages function similarly, with key focal points where actors naturally draw the audience's attention.

As a director, it is crucial to ensure actors cover these areas throughout a scene. Actors should never clump together in one spot for too long, nor should movement feel random. The art of staging is about balance. A Shakespearean scene should have fluidity, but also a deliberate shape that enhances meaning and storytelling, like music that builds and recedes, creating patterns that satisfy the eye and the ear. This reflects the Elizabethan fascination in setting ideas against each other: matching organic forms with formal structures, natural shapes with artifice.

There are exercises to help actors become more aware of stage positioning. Try taping coloured marks on the floor at each of these powerful points, and allowing actors to speak only when moving toward or standing on these marks. Or permit actors to move only when they are speaking but remain still when silent. These exercises encourage them to use the stage dynamically while maintaining variety and clarity. While time constraints in rehearsals often mean such exercises are luxuries, they are useful in developing a sense of spatial awareness that becomes instinctive in performance.

For large scenes with numerous characters or fights or dances or musical numbers, there needs to be very structured blocking. A dance is the most structured of all blocking because everyone is choreographed in time with each other. But then you could argue, well, what's the difference between a dance and a battle? Because, actually, a battle is a kind of dance. Everything is choreographed. No move in dances and battles should happen for the first time in performance; it should always be something you've done before, something your body knows. Then you could ask, well, what's the difference between a dance, a battle and a complex resolution scene at the end of a Shakespeare play where all the characters are on stage? These scenes exist on a continuum.

A resolution scene with fifteen characters at the end of the play requires a lot of structure for it to work consistently and be engaging for the audience. I can tell you from hard experience that those big scenes at the end of Shakespeare plays require a lot of rehearsal time. Start work early in rehearsal, because they are difficult to get running smoothly and can be unsatisfying and even boring if they're not properly thought out. It is critical to ensure every movement is intentional and that the audience's focus is carefully managed throughout the inevitable sequence of revelations, like a conductor guiding an orchestra through a complex finale.

On the other end of the spectrum, you will have intimate scenes between two or three actors. I remember working with two superb actors playing Angelo and Isabella in *Measure for Measure,* Hugh Sexton and Rebecca Rogers. They have two brilliant scenes together that are great fun for the actors to perform, though thematically challenging. The atmosphere of threat, the moral conflict, the struggle for power – all of this demands space for discovery and play. In this case, I left the staging mostly up to them. My job was initially to make sure we all agreed what was happening in the scene, then I simply said, *Let's run it a few times and see where it goes.* Eventually, the scene settled down. We agreed that if they wanted to make small changes to the staging during performance, they should feel free, as long as they weren't throwing their scene partner off too much. They staged it slightly differently every night, and this freedom within constraints led to exciting, living performances. Interestingly, in those scenes both actors played with their connection to the audience, with Isabella eliciting the audience's sympathy through direct addresss, and Angelo largely ignoring them and playing directly to Isabella. In this dynamic, the actor who included the audience gained their moral support against their scene partner.

The freedom for actors to explore within structured guidance is one of the great joys of theatre, the balance between form and spontaneity that keeps the work alive.

The traffic of the stage: transitions and momentum

Entrances and exits matter. Fluid transitions between scenes carry the momentum of the story without pause, without interruption. There is no time for cumbersome set changes, no moments of darkness to reset the world. The stage itself remains fixed whilst the only transformation is in the words, the movement, the energy of the players. This is the traffic of the stage.

In Shakespeare's time, the concept of a full blackout for a transition did not exist. A scene ended, another began immediately. *Exeunt. Enter omnes.* The flow of action remains uninterrupted. Contrast this with some productions where the lights fade, the audience sits in darkness, and stagehands shuffle sets around for minutes at a time. I have attended a Shakespeare production with elaborate realist sets where each scene change took a minute or more, accumulating to a staggering thirty minutes of dead time across the evening. Thirty minutes in which nothing happened, where the audience was forced to disengage, where momentum evaporated. This is the legacy of nineteenth-century realism, a world obsessed with elaborate scenic illusions. But we are not in the nineteenth century. We do not need to bow to this dead tradition.

A crucial rule of Bloody Good Shakespeare: there must never be dead space between scenes. The stage must remain alive. As one scene ends, the next must already be beginning. This does not mean chaotic overlap, but a constant, pulsing rhythm that keeps the play moving. Gaps between scenes drain energy, disengage the audience, and lengthen runtime unnecessarily. Shakespeare's work thrives on pace; directors must honour this by ensuring that the production's heartbeat never falters.

Explore how far you can push the overlap between scenes. It is possible to even run large sections of two overlapping scenes together, playing with which lines are spoken or what business is presented. Experiment in rehearsals is key – be an opportunist looking for the chance to merge scenes in this way.

The director's role: what it is and isn't

A director must know what they are – and are not – responsible for. They are not acting coaches. A director does not teach actors; they *direct* them. Their job is not to improve an actor's craft in general but to shape and guide the best possible performance of *this* play. Actor training is a lifelong pursuit, with dedicated teachers and coaches.

The director's role is different – it is about structure, pacing, and storytelling clarity, not about refining technique. Their responsibility is to safeguard the story, ensure actors look brilliant on stage, and shape unforgettable, spectacular productions. Occasionally, a director may need to offer coaching, but it is rare that they should give line readings. In fact, line readings always do more harm than good – actors tend to get stuck trying to replicate the director's voice rather than making the line their own. Instead, shaping a performance through adjustments in pace, tone, or movement allows for growth while preserving the actor's individuality. The director is more gardener than sculptor – providing the right conditions for growth rather than dictating every detail.

That said, timing can and should be directed. There's nothing wrong with specifying that a pause should last exactly three beats. Performance stress can lead actors to rush lines, so precise timing instructions can be invaluable. Similarly, directing moments of stillness or breath can significantly impact pacing and dramatic effect. These are technical aspects within the director's remit, providing a framework within which the actor can explore.

The best theatre happens when structure and spontaneity coexist. In the early stages of rehearsals, I rarely interfere with how actors deliver their lines. My first priority is ensuring the scene runs – that literally the scene can run from beginning to end without stopping. This invariably exposes other practical problems that can be addressed. Only once the framework is solid is there the potential to refine the emotional and interpretative aspects, ensuring that actors understand their characters' goals and are moving with purpose.

Practical Tips for Directors:

- **Know your play inside out.** If you want actors to trust you, you must have a deep understanding of the text, its structure, and its rhythms. Be prepared to answer any question about motivation, context, or meaning.

- **Create a clear rehearsal structure.** Establish a roadmap for rehearsals. When will you block scenes? When will you shift focus to refining performance? Actors work best with clear expectations.

- **Encourage actors to play.** Early on, let them experiment with different interpretations. Give them permission to fail in rehearsals – it often leads to unexpected brilliance.

- **Direct through questions, not commands.** Instead of saying, *Do it this way*, ask, *What if we try it this way?* This keeps actors engaged in the creative process rather than just taking instructions. *What if...* is one of the most powerful collaborative phrases in the world – use it.

- **Use imagery and metaphor.** Instead of micro-managing an actor's delivery, offer visual or emotional cues. For example, *Imagine you're walking a tightrope in this scene* will be more effective than *Say this line faster*.

- **Know when to step forward.** To get a scene started, it's usually simplest for the director to provide some simple blocking. Then run the scene and see what feedback the actors bring. Blocking *always* changes as rehearsals continue, so you're just providing a simple framework to kick off the process.

- **Know when to step back.** Sometimes, the best directing choice is to let an actor find their own way. Resist the urge to over-direct.

- **Foster unity, hope, and joy.** A strong company culture begins with these three principles. When actors trust one another (*unity*), they take bigger creative risks. When they believe in the work (*hope*), they push through difficulty. When rehearsals are infused with a spirit of play (*joy*), the energy translates directly into performance.

A director must lead. That much is clear. But they must also serve – not in deference, not in passivity, but in a way that places the needs of the production and the company above their own ego. A great director is a *servant leader*, someone who wields their authority not for control, but for creation.

Servant leadership is often misunderstood. Some assume it means stepping back, letting the company lead themselves, or operating by committee. Nothing could be further from the truth. Theatre demands vision, decisiveness, and a firm hand on the tiller. But it also demands trust. A director who hoards power, who dictates rather than collaborates, stifles creativity and breeds disunity, despair and ultimately misery. A director who is indecisive, who abdicates responsibility, creates the same chaos. The balance is everything.

A servant leader in the rehearsal room understands that their job is not to be the loudest voice but to create the conditions where the best work can happen. They provide clarity, direction, and structure while ensuring that every actor, designer, and technician has the freedom to bring their artistry to the fore. They set the tone, not by demanding respect, but by earning it – through preparedness, good humour, deep knowledge of the play, and an ability to inspire through clearly communicating their vision.

At Pop-up Globe, this balance was essential. The nature of our productions – fast-paced, high profile, extremely physical, deeply connected to the audience – meant that actors had to feel empowered to take risks. My job as director was to create a space where those risks could be taken safely. To push actors when they needed pushing. To support them when they wavered. To challenge them to find more, dig deeper, go further. But always in service of the work.

Shakespeare's own company functioned as a tightly bonded ensemble. Their success wasn't built on hierarchy but on trust, collaboration, and shared purpose. The best Shakespearean productions today operate the same way. And the best directors know that their job isn't to be the star – it's to create the conditions where the stars can shine.

Napoleon believed that *a leader is a dealer in hope*. And this is especially true in theatre. A director must instill belief – not just in the work, but in the people bringing it to life. The best directors cultivate an environment where actors feel confident to take risks, where the company trusts the process and each other even in moments of doubt, and where the sheer joy of theatre-making remains at the heart of it all. Leadership in theatre is about inspiration. It's about ensuring that, on opening night, every person on that stage steps forward knowing they are an essential and appreciated part of something remarkable.

Working with actors: the art of the offer

Find the best actors you possibly can. Bloody good actors make for Bloody Good Shakespeare. Hold open auditions, go to good productions and see if you can talk to individual actors afterwards. Don't be nervous, it's naturally very flattering for actors to be in demand. You will be surprised, particularly if you talk with joy and hope about your plans. If the company is already provided, I strongly recommend meeting with your leads individually prior to rehearsal to share your vision and make sure they are on board with you and your process.

Rehearsal is a space of possibility, an arena in which the actor must come armed with ideas, ideas that can be discarded, reshaped, layered, built upon. This is the essence of the actor's craft: to bring offers.

An offer is a gesture of creativity. It is the moment an actor steps forward not to ask, *What do you want?* but to say, *What about this?* It is movement, voice, rhythm, silence; it is a risk. And in this, the actor and the director meet in true collaboration. The great mistake is to imagine that the director is the sculptor and the actor merely the clay. The good director is not an architect of fixed ideas, handing down decrees from a throne. The good director is an editor, a guide, a fellow traveller in the discovery of the actor's performance in service of the story.

At Pop-up Globe, I saw two kinds of actors. There were those who entered the space brimming with offers, full of invention, free of attachment to any single idea. These actors were playful, fluid, ready to be wrong, ready to try again. Their suggestions might be brilliant, they might be foolish, but that did not matter; the rehearsal was alive because of them. And then there were those who waited. Those who sought instruction rather than exploration, who looked to the director for the right answer. These actors were not without skill, but they had not yet understood that the best performances are never handed down, they are discovered in the act of doing.

I have always found my greatest joy in working with the first kind of actor. The actor who knows that an offer is not precious, that a discarded idea is not a failure but an invitation to another. There is no fear in this kind of work, no ego in being 'right', only the thrill of uncovering what was not there before. These actors use the director in the best way possible, as a mirror, as a challenge, as an amplifier for what they bring. And the result is a performance that is owned, inhabited, alive. The audience feels this authenticity; they know when an actor is truly present in the moment, not simply executing instructions.

When an actor does not bring offers, the director is left to invent for them. And this is always lesser. A performance imposed from without, no matter how well-executed, will never have the same truth as one that has been forged from within. The audience can feel this. They can sense the difference between a moment that is lived and one that is prescribed. This is why Shakespeare's theatre, a theatre of immediacy, a theatre where the actor speaks directly to the audience, demands actors who bring themselves fully into the process.

With actors who are less confident, you may have to give them staging in rehearsal that they can later hang their performance on. Introduce games actors can play on stage to help them move past their sense of imposter syndrome. Maybe one actor has something they need to give the other actor, or take from them. Tell one actor their job is to make the other actor look at them, while the other actor's job is to avoid eye contact. These games open up opportunities. Another useful technique is introducing obstacles in movement: a chair between them, a prop they have to hide, or an action they must complete during the conversation. These small adjustments bring authenticity to the scene and in turn can spark more discovery. Physical tasks often unlock emotional truths that intellectual discussion cannot reach.

Rehearsal, then, is not about finding the one way, but about testing many. It is about generosity. It is about stepping forward, again and again, to say: *What if...* It is about creating a space where failure is not only acceptable but necessary, where each attempt brings you closer to the truth of the play, even if that truth is different from what you initially imagined.

I think it's great to bring props into the rehearsal room as soon as possible, along with elements of costume. They don't need to be the final versions (stand-ins are fine), but if an actor is going to wear a hat, get them used to wearing a hat. If they'll carry a sword, even if it's a cardboard sword, get it into rehearsals early. Familiarity with props and costumes helps actors integrate them naturally into performance rather than treating them as foreign objects on opening night. Physicalising these elements early in rehearsal means actors are free to focus on performance rather than adapting to new elements late in the process. Avoid giving actors a heavy cloak or an unwieldy prop in the final week, completely disrupting the performance they've been building.

It's critical for the entire company to have plenty of opportunity to see the play run as rehearsals develop. When I directed *A Midsummer Night's Dream*, every Friday afternoon we ran the play, stumbling through as-yet-unstaged scenes and showing the work left to do. And while I wouldn't necessarily repeat that experiment, it's absolutely the case that running the play allows actors to learn its rhythm, recognise where pacing needs to shift, and refine the transitions that bring the whole piece together. Shakespeare's plays find their full voice through performance, not discussion, and repeated runs amplify that voice. Each run reveals new insights, new problems to solve, new opportunities to explore.

Many theatre companies do not dedicate enough time to running the play before an audience arrives, meaning that the first few performances are where the actors figure out the show's pacing. This is a shame because it forces paying audiences to watch a production still finding its footing. Ensuring the play has been run enough times before the first public performance means that actors are confident in its movement, rhythm, and timing, allowing them to focus on playing rather than damage control. The greater familiarity an actor has with the overall structure of the play, the more comfortable they will be in delivering their best work with freedom and precision. This confidence is the foundation of truly inspired performance.

Why simplicity matters in staging Shakespeare

One of the greatest threats to a Shakespeare production is an overcomplicated technical setup, particularly elaborate lighting plots. Too much reliance on intricate lighting can slow down runs and delay rehearsals. For a Shakespeare production, where clarity of storytelling and performance is paramount, it's worth considering how much technical complexity is truly necessary. Technology should serve the story, not the other way around.

A large-scale modern theatre production with heavy technical demands follows a rigid, time-consuming process that often prioritizes precision over spontaneity. First, there's a paper tech, where the technical team and stage management discuss every lighting cue, sound cue, automation move, and projection shift. Then comes the dry tech, where lights, sound, and automation cues are run without actors to check timings and transitions. After that, the company moves into technical rehearsals, which can last a week or more. These are long, grueling days – actors stand around waiting while cues are set and adjusted, often getting through only a few minutes of the play in many hours. Then comes cue-to-cue, stopping and starting repeatedly to refine transitions. Finally, dress rehearsals attempt a full run, but technical issues often mean more stops and resets.

For high-tech proscenium musicals, this process is essential. But does Shakespeare benefit from it? Absolutely not. Elaborate lighting states and electronic effects don't enhance the work – they obscure it and slow it down. Pop-up Globe's fixed set and universal lighting meant we gained back valuable rehearsal time. While other productions spent days in stop-start technical rehearsals, we used our time in the playhouse prior to the opening night running the show multiple times, refining performances, improving transitions, deepening character work, and ensuring clarity of storytelling. The actors became sharper, more responsive, more attuned to the audience. Without the distraction of unnecessary technical complexity, the play itself could be worked hard and taken to the next level, ready for the audience.

The living play

In summary: get the play on its feet as quickly as possible. Avoid sitting around a table discussing it endlessly; stage it, run it, refine it. You cannot improve a play until you can see it as a living, breathing entity. Build an ensemble that works together to tell the story dynamically, ensuring that the entire company is engaged in making the play as rich as possible. Above all, foster trust by speaking less and letting the actors act. The best rehearsal room is one where the work speaks louder than the director. It is through movement, interaction, and the natural chemistry of the cast that the play begins to reveal its full potential.

The actors who truly succeed in Shakespearean performance are the ones who embrace the unpredictability of live theatre. They listen intently, respond dynamically, and allow the energy of the space to shape their work. The audience feels this electricity, this sense of being present at something unique and fleeting.

As directors, our role is to guide, not dictate; to shape, not control. We provide structure, but within that structure, we must leave room for spontaneity, discovery, and, above all, play. When actors feel free, when they trust the world we have built together, the magic happens. That magic is what brings the text alive, making it accessible and meaningful to audiences today.

And that magic is what theatre is all about. We rehearse not to create something perfect, but to create something alive and repeatable. If we succeed, then by the time the audience arrives, they join us in a riot, a revelation, an experience that feels as fresh and unpredictable as the day it was first performed.

Top: *The author works from Auckland Library's copy of the First Folio and other editions in preparing the performance script of* Twelfth Night *in Auckland, 2015. Bottom: Actors Adrian Hooke and Joel Herbert lift Chris Huntly-Turner as Henry V in open-air rehearsals at Ellerslie, Auckland, 2017. The Auckland Pop-up Globe playhouse is visible in the background.*

Top: Actor Rawiri Paratene (left), the author (centre) and Head of Stage Combat & Special Effects Alex Holloway in rehearsals for Henry V, Pop-up Globe Auckland, 2017. Bottom: The Exeter's Company in rehearsals for the transfer of Twelfth Night to Pop-up Globe Perth in 2019. Note the use of stand-in costumes to help accustom actors to the scale and feel of their performance costumes.

Top: Finishing touches are made to actors costumes on stage during a notes session prior to a performance of A Midsummer Night's Dream by the Exeter's Company at Pop-up Globe Perth, 2019. Bottom: The women of the Nottingham's Company are led in song by Summer Millet (Mariana) at a dress rehearsal for Measure For Measure at Pop-up Globe Perth, 2019.

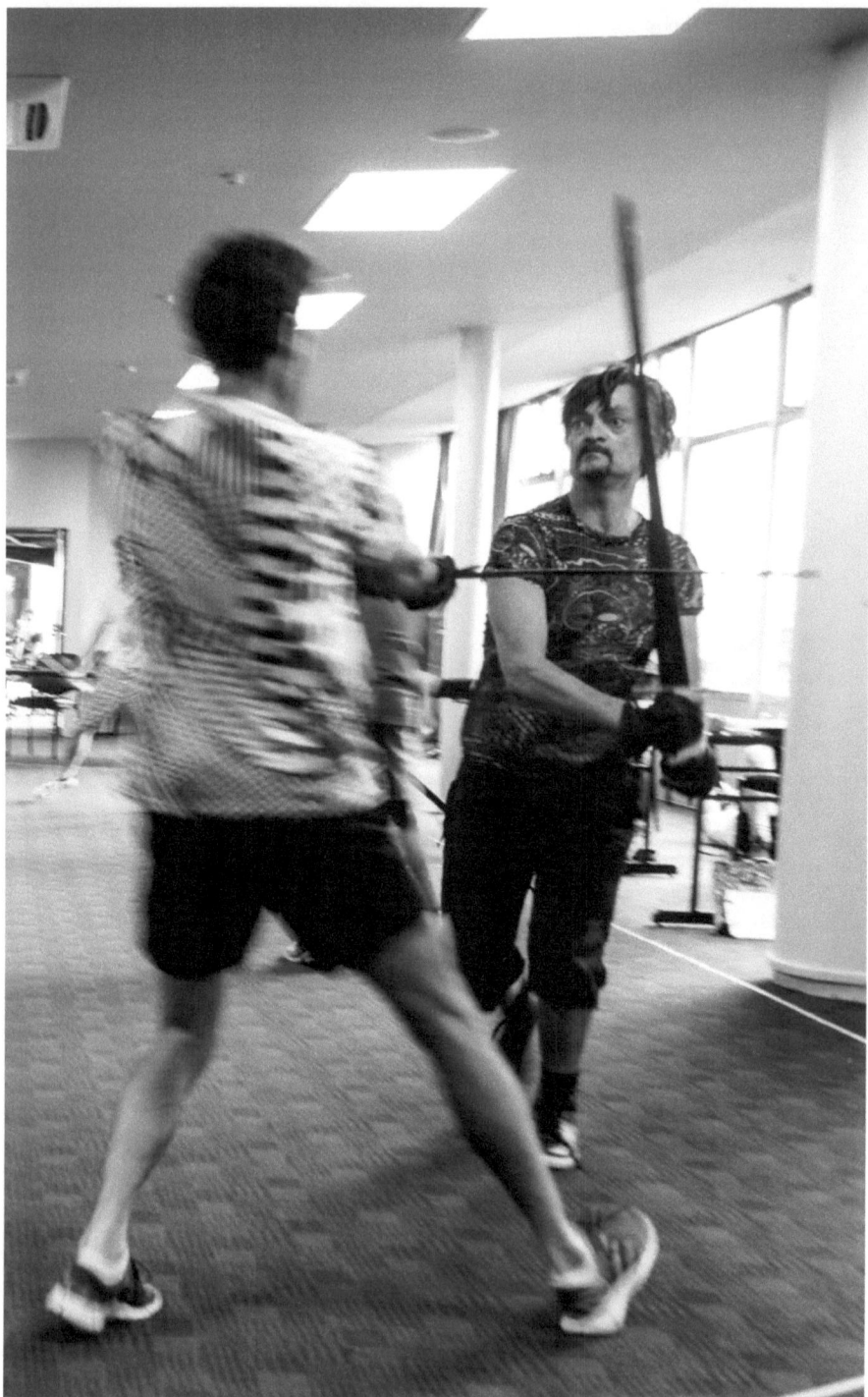

Stephen Butterworth of the King's Company in fight rehearsals for Henry V, Pop-up Globe Auckland, 2017. All actors needed to be physically fit and in good shape for the intense demands of Bloody Good Shakespeare.

Māori actor Reuben Butler (Puck) flies through the air during rehearsals for the Buckingham's bi-lingual A Midsummer Night's Dream at Pop-up Globe Auckland, 2017. The fairies were portrayed as Patupaiarehe, ancient Māori fairy creatures. Most of Puck, Oberon and Titania's lines were translated into Te Reo Māori by acclaimed Māori poet Pierre Lyndon.

The Alchemy of Spectacle

SHAKESPEARE'S THEATRE IS A theatre of spectacle, of visual splendour. He understood spectacle as a necessity, as something fundamental to the storytelling itself. To direct Shakespeare without acknowledging this is to rob the plays of their vitality.

Spectacle is to the eyes what music is to the ears. Whether through the clang of swords, the hiss of an arrow, the spray of blood or the immense joy of a final dance, it is the physicality of theatre that transforms it from something observed to something experienced. Pursue spectacle. Because spectacle + emotion = Bloody Good Shakespeare.

Spectacle and emotion exist together, one shaping the other. A fireworks display will always elicit a reaction – *oohs* and *aahs* from the crowd – but without emotional meaning, it is a fleeting sensation, a momentary wonder. The true power of spectacle lies in its ability to expand story. A fight, a dance, a storm – they captivate when they are charged with emotion. Audiences understand this instinctively. They do not come to watch Shakespeare for words alone. They come for the full experience: the music, the movement, the blood, the battles, the wonder. And they come to see a world that is bigger, bolder, more dangerous than their own.

But how can we create spectacle if we remove elaborate scenery, if we strip away the electronic tricks of modern 'West End Theatre'? The answer is that every other element must work harder. A fixed set, or no set at all, immediately places enormous responsibility on all other elements of the production.

Naturally, costumes and props become more important. How the actors' bodies are clothed becomes critical. Costumes must be spectacular, visually arresting. They must tell the story, elevate the world of the play, heighten reality. Every design, every fabric choice, must be deliberate, must add something – whether it be historical veracity or a bold, theatrical abstraction that captures the essence of a character before they have even spoken.

The audience reads objects differently in an environment stripped of unnecessary clutter. A prop must be purposeful, meaningful. A sword, a letter, a cup – each one must be a tool not just for function but for storytelling. The weight of a crown in *Richard III*, the eerie presence of Yorick's skull in *Hamlet*, the dagger in *Macbeth* – these are more than objects. They are symbols, charged with narrative force. If we are to discard set changes, if we are to reject the trappings of realism, then the few physical items we do choose must carry an enormous weight. I will return to the importance of hand props and their storytelling journey in the next chapter.

Beyond costume and props, the action of the stage – movement, fights, dances, ritual, magic – becomes key in the creation of spectacle.

The art of violence

Fight direction is not choreography in the way a ritual dance is. It is not about aesthetic perfection but about truth. The best fights are the ones that reveal something. A duel should tell you more about the two humans fighting than any line of text. How they fight matters more than what they fight with. Are they trained? Are they desperate? Are they afraid? Do they hesitate? An experienced warrior fights differently from a youth forced into violence for the first time. Violence is an expression of character, of individual experience.

I had the good fortune to work for many years with the passionate and talented Alexander Holloway, Head of Stage Combat and Special Effects throughout Pop-up Globe's existence. His dedication to research and precision brought Shakespeare's spectacle to life. In the ghostly presence of his father, Hamlet's sword burst into flame. Thanks to him, Richard III did not just speak of war – he waged it before the audience's eyes. In *Henry V*, cannons fired, the theatre shook with their sound, and the air was thick with the smell of gunpowder. And then there were the flaming arrows. Fired from the upper levels of the theatre by members of the ensemble armed with bows, they soared across the audience on zip wires, cutting through the charged air before striking the set. And there, in full sight, a stage manager rushed to extinguish them, the act of putting out the flame becoming part of the performance itself. The audience did not merely watch a battle; they were inside it.

Alex taught me that a fight is a form of punctuation, a physical exclamation mark. It is transformation. It changes relationships, alters power dynamics, forces the characters – and the audience – to see things differently. This is why timing is critical. A fight that is too slow, too careful, loses its impact and drains energy from the stage. A fight that is too fast becomes a blur and can become truly dangerous. The balance must be struck. Every beat must be felt, every movement must have purpose.

The best fight scenes are not necessarily the grandest. Sometimes, the smallest acts of violence contain the most weight. A slap, a struggle, a sudden, unexpected movement – these can be more shocking than any sword fight. On stage, we must find a way to balance the reality of that with the heightened theatrical world we are creating. Consider the horrible intimacy of violence in the last moments before death at the hands of another. Do not shy away from these brutal realities.

Because violence in Shakespeare is rarely clean. It is rarely heroic. It is more often cowardly, tragic. In *Macbeth*, the violence spirals out of control, each act leading to the next, until there is no way back. In *Othello*, the final act is suffocating, not just because of what happens but because of how inevitable it feels. The best fight direction understands this. It does not treat fights as isolated events but as part of the larger structure of the play.

Violence must have consequences. Too often, fight scenes are treated as technical showcases – opportunities for actors to display their training. But if the fight does not change something – if it does not leave a scar, physically or emotionally – then what was the point? Every act of violence shifts the world of the play. If it doesn't, it should not be there.

There is space for comedy within violence. Think of the fight in *Bridget Jones's Diary*, a messy, graceless, almost comic scrap between two middle-aged men who have no idea what they are doing. It is brilliant because it is honest. In *Henry V*, we gave the Chorus a mop, and he fought the French with it. The audience loved it. Real fights are not ballet. They are awkward, painful, desperate, intimate. A fight scene does not always have to be grim; it only needs to be true to the reality unfolding on stage. Violence can be absurd, humiliating, ridiculous, just as much as it can be terrifying. Let the context and characters be your guide.

Fight direction requires time. Too often, it is started too late, or even worse, squeezed into the final rehearsals. This is a mistake. Combat must be embedded in the body, rehearsed with the same care as any spoken line. This is why working with professionals is essential. A great fight director does not just teach actors how to swing a sword; they teach them how to fight for their lives. They make the danger feel real while keeping the actors safe. The best fights are the ones that feel as though they could go wrong at any moment – but never do. The audience should never doubt the skill behind the scene, but they should also never see it.

At Pop-up Globe, we embraced this fully. Every fight was treated as a real fight. Every sword was drawn with intention. Blood was spilled. When violence erupted, it meant something. The battles, the music, the jigs, the wild eruptions of blood and fire were the pulse of the work itself. We staged battles with bodies, not abstractions. In *Richard III* and *Henry V*, the field of battle was filled with actors in full armour, clashing, falling, rising again. No metaphors. Just steel, sweat, and urgency.

The blood revelation: a turning point

We learned the power of blood very early in our adventure with the Pop-up Globe. It happened during the first preview of Ben Naylor's production of *Romeo and Juliet* in February 2016, and it transformed our understanding of theatrical experience forever.

Everything was going beautifully that night. The house was two-thirds full – almost all lawyers and their families, corporate guests of our generous sponsors Anthony Harper. They sat in their seats, polite, attentive. The yard was empty, as the corporate audience sat in the galleries, unwilling to stand to watch. Only one child stood in the yard, right up against the stage. This boy had the best view in the theatre.

The fights were tight, the actors on fire, the tension electric. And then, in Act 3, Scene i, the moment that should have been our triumph became something else entirely.

Tybalt and Mercutio fought, and the blades flashed. Gasps from the crowd. The fatal blow landed. Mercutio staggered from the stage, blood pouring from his stomach and mouth. Romeo, grief-stricken, turned to face Tybalt. They fought. The final thrust. Tybalt gasped. And then – the blood bag burst.

It had been planned, of course. A perfect pop, a cup or so of blood, spattering upstage to complete the visual shock of Tybalt's murder. But something went wrong. Instead of bursting upstage, safely contained, it shot forward, spraying down into the yard.

Onto the child.

The boy, no older than eleven, standing at the very front, directly in the line of fire. His face was covered in blood. Like a horror movie.

On stage, the actors froze. The audience inhaled as one. From where I stood, watching in horror, I saw his parents – lawyers, remember – sitting bolt upright. A thousand thoughts hit me at once. *We will be sued. This will be the end of us. The theatre will close before it has even begun. The child is traumatised. His therapy bills will bankrupt us.*

But the play must go on. Somehow, it did. The first half ended. Our front-of-house team rushed forward, towels and a free T-shirt in hand, ready to apologise, ready to beg forgiveness.

And the boy?

He turned, eyes wide, blood dripping, grinning ear to ear.

That was the best thing that's ever happened to me!

He was ecstatic. His father laughed, shaking his head. No lawsuit. No angry front-of-house complaints. Just joy. Pure, unexpected, visceral joy.

And then something extraordinary happened. As the interval stretched on, the lawyers and their families began leaving their seats. They drifted down from the galleries, stepping into the yard, crowding closer to the stage.

They wanted to be hit by the blood too.

The visceral theatre: blood as connection

It was a revelation. Until that moment, we had tried to contain the blood, to keep it controlled, to limit its reach. But theatre – true theatre – does not want to be contained. From that night on, we changed everything. Blood was no longer a problem to manage but a gift to the audience. We let it fly. We aimed for the yard. People wanted to be part of the spectacle.

Blood was no longer just an effect. It was an experience. It bound the audience to the play, made them complicit, made them feel the cost of violence in a way no neat, bloodless death ever could. It was a risk. It was messy. It was real. The groundlings at Pop-up Globe did not just see the theatre; they felt it, smelled it, wore it.

Blood is necessary. Without blood, violence is an idea, an abstraction, a thing of no danger. And Shakespeare's theatre, above all, should be dangerous.

But when blood does flow, it must be glorious. And it should expand beyond the confines of the stage, into the crowd.

It's more than just blood, of course. When the porter in *Macbeth* relieved himself with careless abandon off the stage and onto the spectators, when the drunken vicar in *As You Like It* lost the contents of his stomach at an unfortunate moment straight onto the groundlings (this moment is pictured at the end of this chapter), or old Adam had his teeth knocked out by a punch and scattered across the yard – these acts were part of the immersive contract of shared space.

At first, there were concerns. Would audiences complain? Would we face a sea of dry-cleaning bills? But as it turned out, the answer was simple: warn them, and they will embrace it. A simple sign at the entrance, a knowing smile from an usher, and soon enough, you could see it – the delighted anticipation in the eyes of those at the front, waiting, hoping for the moment when the play would break its own frame and reach out to touch them. And when it came – in whatever form – the reaction was immediate. Laughter. Gasps. That exquisite mixture of horror and glee. It doesn't detract from the moment, it heightens it.

In our second season, when Henry V cut the Constable's throat at the climax of the battle of Agincourt, the audience saw a full-bodied arc, a crimson ribbon stretching out across the yard. The ones who were hit reeled back, gasping, half in shock, half in delight. And then the laughter – wild, disbelieving, electric. They looked at themselves, at their hands, their shirts, at the thick red mess now a part of them, and for that moment, they were not simply watching theatre. They were living history.

And the ones who weren't hit? They felt it too. They laughed uneasily, touched their necks, instinctively, a hand rising without thought to check that their own throats were still intact. And then, as if reassured, as if emboldened, they edged forward, deeper into the action, hungrier for the next moment.

That moment, when the blood flew up to six metres from the stage, when the noise in the theatre swelled like a coliseum baying for more, was something no other art form can replicate. You can see these reactions in the images taken during *Henry V* at the end of this chapter.

When Julius Caesar was struck down in Rita Stone's 2018 production, the daggers flashed, the robes stained red, the conspirators and audience were drenched in the bloody ruin of their own making. The audience did not simply watch – they witnessed. They left the theatre with the imprint of that image behind their eyes, and the legacy of it drying on their t-shirts.

It is this, more than anything, that proves what I have always believed: Shakespearean theatre should never feel safe. It should happen *to* you, not *at* you. The audience should not simply observe – they should be affected. They should leave the theatre changed, physically and psychologically.

The practical realities of blood

For all its glorious impact on stage, blood backstage is a nightmare. It stains, it smears, it sticks where you don't want it, and it spreads where you least expect it. I have seen actors step onto the stage confidently, only to find their footing suddenly treacherous, a slick of fake blood turning solid ground into ice. I have seen costumes ruined beyond repair, linen stiffened into unwearable sheets, boots that squelch with each step.

We learned quickly that the practicalities matter enormously. Blood spatters have to be carefully controlled – not just for maximum effect, but to avoid pooling where an actor might later plant their foot. The stage has to be wiped between scenes, rags concealed or even worn by the right characters for quick mopping. Costumes have to be duplicated if blood is used early in the show – there is nothing worse than an actor returning for a later scene looking as though they've already been murdered.

The wooden stage of the Pop-up Globe, like the boards of Shakespeare's own Globe, absorbed the history of performances into itself. In Shakespeare's time, they likely used animal blood from the butcher's yard – cheap, abundant, real. It would have seeped into the grain, darkened the rushes and planks, left a smell that clung long after the play was done. It is impossible to imagine that they worried about staining. The stage was a place of life and death, and death leaves its mark.

Some of our audiences left looking as though they had fought in a battle themselves. And isn't that right? The Battle of Agincourt should not be something we admire from a safe distance. Shakespeare gives us the rousing speeches, yes, but he also gives us the bodies, the dirt, the brutality. The audience, spattered and gasping, were not merely spectators. They had lived as soldiers in Henry's army. They had fought and won at Agincourt.

Sound and music: the heart of emotion

The best sound effects are live, expanding from the text, mechanically produced in the space there and then. A trumpet fanfare. A distant sound of wind chimes. A beating drum – now a heartbeat, now a distant warning. Humming breaking into song.

And then there are the cannons. I have always loved the potential of sound in theatre. A cannon does not simply mark a moment; it tears through it. Shakespeare's own company fired them in *Henry VIII* – one misfire, and the Globe burned to the ground. That is the risk of real spectacle. That is the thrill. We did not burn down Pop-up Globe, but we did fire cannons, and every time they went off, you felt them in your chest, in your bones. They announced war. They announced death. They told the audience: wake up, something is happening.

These are the kind of effects it's worth spending technical time on. They can be honed, and made brilliant in rehearsal. They take Shakespeare in performance to the next level.

Music, with its remarkable ability to transport, enchant, or even overwhelm a listener, drawing them out of themselves in rapture, is the very breath of the theatre. Acoustic, always acoustic. Instruments in the hands of the actors themselves, or dedicated musicians present on stage. A drumbeat that underscores a scene, a sudden burst of song that shifts the tone entirely. And of course, the voice – actors trained not just to speak, but to sing, to let the resonance of their own bodies shape the soundscape of the play. A production that relies on recorded music is a production that has forgotten the primal nature of performance.

When we built Pop-up Globe, we built a space that demanded music. A theatre with no amplified sound, where every note had to cut through air thick with voices and bodies, where rhythm was not a private experience between musician and instrument but something that had to fill the space, drive the play forward, strike the audience at their core. And at the heart of this musical life was Paul McLaney, our director of music.

I met Paul over lunch when Pop-up Globe was still only an idea, a dream that had yet to be built. He spoke of the sonnets, of setting them to music, of lifting their words from the page and making them sing. A poet, a composer, a man with an instinct not just for melody but for meaning – Paul became the architect of the sound of Pop-up Globe. He composed for *Romeo and Juliet*, for *Twelfth Night*, for play after play after play. It was when he stood on stage in that first season, playing in the band, that something changed in him. He was no longer just writing for the theatre – he was living it, within it, feeling its pulse with every performance. That intimacy shaped everything that followed.

It is not enough to place a song where a song is written, to herald an entrance with a flourish and consider the job done. Music must run deeper than that. Underscore as you see fit, saving this for moments of focus. A subtle line of sound beneath a monologue, a swell of music to meet an entrance, the quietest note at the moment of revelation. We discovered that music, carefully placed, could direct the audience's attention and emotion with exquisite power.

In Māori director Miriama McDowell's thrilling, Pasifika-infused production of *Much Ado About Nothing* at Pop-up Globe, audience engagement was sung into being. First staged in Auckland in 2017, the action was vividly relocated to a banana plantation, with Dogberry (Kieran Mortell) and Verges

(Johnny Light) reimagined as customs officers, hilariously tasked with ensuring no illegal or dangerous produce entered the island.

One of the production's most powerful moments unfolded in the scene where Benedick, played by the gifted Semu Filipo, sang to the Gods of Love. As his voice lifted in invocation, he invited the audience to hum in tune. What began as a gentle vibration through the space became a collective harmony, as Semu soared above the growing resonance of hundreds of humming voices. This was true collective storytelling, almost sacral. It was a reminder that theatre, at its most alive, breaks the fourth wall not with gimmickry but with generosity. That moment of shared music was was emotionally irresistible, transforming spectators into co-creators in the dramatic spell. A simple act of humming became a powerful act of communion, binding actor and audience in a single, sustained breath of theatrical magic.

And as the years went on, the music grew. More and more, I found myself structuring productions around it. We opened acts with song; we closed them with dance. In *Henry V*, the first half ended with the entire company returning to the stage, still stained with the grime of war, to sing Marlowe's words: *Blood is the God of War's rich livery... Cursed be those that first invented war...* I remember the moment vividly, the weight of it, the hush of an audience unprepared for that kind of raw simplicity. Music could do that. Music could make war feel immediate, unglorified, real.

By the time we reached *Measure for Measure*, the integration of music was absolute. We began in song, the company raising their voices together, grounding the world of the play before a single line had been spoken. We ended in dance, but a dance that was not just a final bow, not just a tradition, but something essential – something drawn from the movement of the play itself, an extension of its themes, its contradictions, its unresolved tensions.

The mistake so often made is to bring music in too late, to treat it as an addition, something that can be slotted in once the work is done. But music, if it is to serve the play, must be part of its bones from the very beginning. The composer must be a collaborator, a co-creator, embedded in the process from the first rehearsals.

And beyond the musicians, beyond the instruments, there is the space itself. Paul McLaney called Pop-up Globe an 'empathy drum', a structure designed not just to contain performance but to amplify it, to resonate with it, to beat in time with the emotion of those within it. The building itself becomes a musical instrument, one that the actors play upon as much as they play upon their lines.

Movement: the life of the text

I have been fortunate to work with extraordinary movement directors, but my longest collaboration was with Brigid Costello, who served as Head of Movement at Pop-up Globe. Brigid understood something fundamental – all movement is storytelling.

Shakespeare's world was a world of dance. In Elizabethan society, dance was more than entertainment. It was power, politics, seduction, ritual. So Shakespeare filled his plays with dance, and ended his plays at the Globe with a jig. In Shakespeare's theatre, the jig was in fact more than a dance. It was a bawdy, riotous, often improvised spectacle, usually led by the clown. It was a show *after* the show, a wild parody, sometimes running for twenty minutes or more. We talked about doing a 'proper' jig at Pop-up Globe, but in the end we settled for a dance that reflected the action of the production, something that, perhaps, captured the spirit of the jig without imitating it.

So at the end of every Pop-up Globe show, we danced. A two- or three-minute explosion of movement, rhythm, and energy, impossible to resist. The audience never failed to clap along. They couldn't help themselves. We tried, once or twice, to control it, to keep the rhythm purely our own. But what a foolish notion that was. The audience was part of it, *had* to be part of it. So we embraced them. We let the dance be theirs as much as ours. The physicality of the moment transcended the text, binding the audience and actors in a shared, almost ritualistic release of energy. It was both a celebration and a farewell.

But the dance was not without its challenges. The sheer volume of the clapping and cheering crowd made it impossible for the actors to hear the music. The solution was simple, essential – *a big drum*. A heartbeat beneath the chaos, a sound that could cut through the noise and give the actors something solid to move against. Thanks to legendary Pop-up Globe musician Oscar West, we discovered that bagpipes helped too – anything with force, with presence, with a sound that could not be drowned. The jig may have belonged to the whole theatre, but the rhythm *had* to hold.

And why stop at one dance? It is my belief now that every Shakespeare production should have four or even more. One early in the play, to set the tone, to draw the audience into the world. One before the interval, to send them buzzing into the break. One to start the second half, to shift the energy, to bring fresh life. And then, of course, the final dance – to send them out exhilarated, full of breath and rhythm and joy.

Movement in a Shakespeare company extends from dance choreography to large-scene blocking, individual actor/character choices through to specialist movement to portray animals or spirits. But it's also about survival. An actor who is not conditioned, who does not prepare their body, will not last through a Shakespeare season. Warm-ups before rehearsals, warm-downs after performances are necessities. Actors need stamina, agility, breath control. This can be the difference between thriving and breaking down.

Ceremony and spectacle

Shakespeare's world was one of ceremony, of formality, of ritual. His plays reflect that. Processions, feasts, coronations, duels. Just as they are today, rituals are moments where meaning is made, either through the ritual's success or failure. They are opportunities, not obstacles. A director who ignores them, who treats them as mere staging problems, is missing something fundamental. These moments are the theatre at its fullest, at its most spectacular. They are the moments where change happens, where we do not just watch – we witness. And in the best productions, we participate.

When we staged *Richard III*, we began the second half with a coronation, a full, resplendent, theatrical act of power. Richard's ascent to the throne was built moment by moment, with every actor, every stage manager, every body we could muster pressed into ensemble service. It became a grand procession, a ritual weighted with significance. The orb, the mace, the crown – each object placed with deliberate care, each movement drawing on the deep well of research we had undertaken to reconstruct the visual language of kingship. The music swelled. The three trumpeters sounded. The world held its breath. This was theatre at its most potent, where ceremony became story, where the physical objects of power told us as much as the words themselves.

And then... the fumble.

In rehearsal, when the Archbishop of Canterbury moved to place the crown on Richard's head, his hands failed him. The crown slipped, teetered, and for a single, heart-stopping moment, it seemed it would crash to the ground. Instinctively, everyone watching reacted. And in that moment, we knew: this must stay. So, every night, the fumble became part of the coronation. Not exaggerated, not clownish, but played just enough that the audience felt the precariousness of it. The moment before Richard becomes king is a moment where it almost doesn't happen. And in that instant, the theatre tightened. The illusion of control wavered. The audience, held in that flickering uncertainty, leaned in. These moments – these fake mistakes, these carefully controlled accidents – inject a pulse of the unpredictable into theatre. They force the audience to believe because they seem to break the frame of performance itself.

A planned, controlled slip – brilliantly executed, at the right moment – makes the stage action feel even more real. There is something primal about it, something that convinces the audience that this is not just stagecraft, not just a story being told at a safe distance, but something immediate, something uncontrolled, something with a physical reality that cannot be ignored. And in that moment the audience forgets everything else, and simply lives in the moment with us.

Shakespeare's company must have known this. They worked in an unrailed, crowded space, packed with moving bodies and shifting ground. They knew how to use the stage beneath them, how to turn a stumble into intention, how to let the hazards of performance feed the drama. A well-placed slip in *Julius Caesar* – a conspirator recoiling too fast from the body, scrambling backward, hands covered in blood – only deepens the horror of the act. A soldier falling in *Henry V*, struggling up as the battle rages, reminds us that war is not heroic posturing but exhaustion, chaos, chance.

But this only works when the actor knows how to fall. A slip must be felt, not faked. If an actor flails too theatrically, the moment is lost, and the audience laughs for the wrong reason. But when the fall is honest – when it happens in the right moment, in the right way – it has the ring of truth. And that, in theatre, is gold.

Ceremony on stage carries challenges as well as power. These are opportunities for grandeur, but they are also traps. Consider the banquet in *Macbeth*. The moment is charged, haunted, but the staging presents a danger: everyone sits, and the energy drops. Sight lines are lost. The air, so thick with tension, risks stagnation. A feast that does not move is a feast that deadens. The same is true in *Hamlet* – diplomatic meetings, funerals, acts of state. These moments carry weight, but weight alone is not enough. They must breathe. They must be alive. They must be shaped with rhythm, with movement, with music and dance, with the pulse of something just beneath the surface.

And it is not just movement – it is contrast. Processions must be grand, but they must also be broken by human moments. The stately entry of a monarch means more if a servant scrambles behind, struggling with a fallen sash. A funeral procession means more if, somewhere in the crowd, a mourner lets out a single, ragged breath, a sob barely stifled. The audience is not moved by the spectacle alone – they are moved when they sense something real struggling beneath it.

The key is detail. Ritual, when done well, holds an audience spellbound, but when left to sprawl, it becomes a history lesson, a tableau, something to be admired rather than experienced. The solution? Precision. Awe. A relentless attention to how these moments land. Music must be felt in the bones, movement must have intention, stillness must hold a crackling tension. The moment must be earned.

The living theatre

Shakespeare's theatre is a theatre where the body must do as much work as the word. The best productions of his plays breathe with the urgency of real life unfolding before us. Without movement, without spectacle, without the sheer physical commitment of the performers, the work risks becoming a recitation rather than an event.

Spectacle, properly used, does not distract from the story – it is the story. When a king is crowned, we must feel the weight of history pressing down upon him, not just in his words but in the way the crown is placed upon his head, the way the court kneels, the way the trumpets blare and echo through the wooden rafters. When a battle is fought, it cannot be reduced to metaphor, to an abstraction of war – it must be bodies clashing, blades flashing, the thud of armour meeting flesh. The audience must not just see it. They must feel it.

And yet, for all its grandeur, the most powerful spectacle can come in the smallest moments. A single actor, standing alone, holding the space in silence. A glance exchanged across a crowded stage, heavy with meaning. The pause before a sword is drawn. These, too, are spectacle. These, too, are the moments that make theatre an act of presence rather than an act of remembering.

The best productions feel as though they are happening for the first time, right now, in front of you. The audience must never know what will come next. This is as true for spectacle as it is for speech. A fight must never feel rehearsed, just as a line must never feel recited. A storm must be a storm, not just an idea of one. Music must be heard, and seen to be made. Blood must be spilled, and it must be shocking. The moment theatre becomes safe, it dies.

We found the more we worked with Shakespeare, the more we felt he invited us to go further with every new show. Our productions were not polite, not restrained, not bound by the timid reverence that so often kills Shakespeare. They were full-blooded, full-throated, alive with the sweat of battle and the rhythm of dance.

The best theatre does not hold the audience at a distance. It reaches out and touches them – sometimes literally, with the blood of a freshly slain soldier spraying across the yard. Those audience members, stunned, laughing at the shock of it, moving closer so that it gets them next time – were *in* the play in a way no cinema screen can ever replicate.

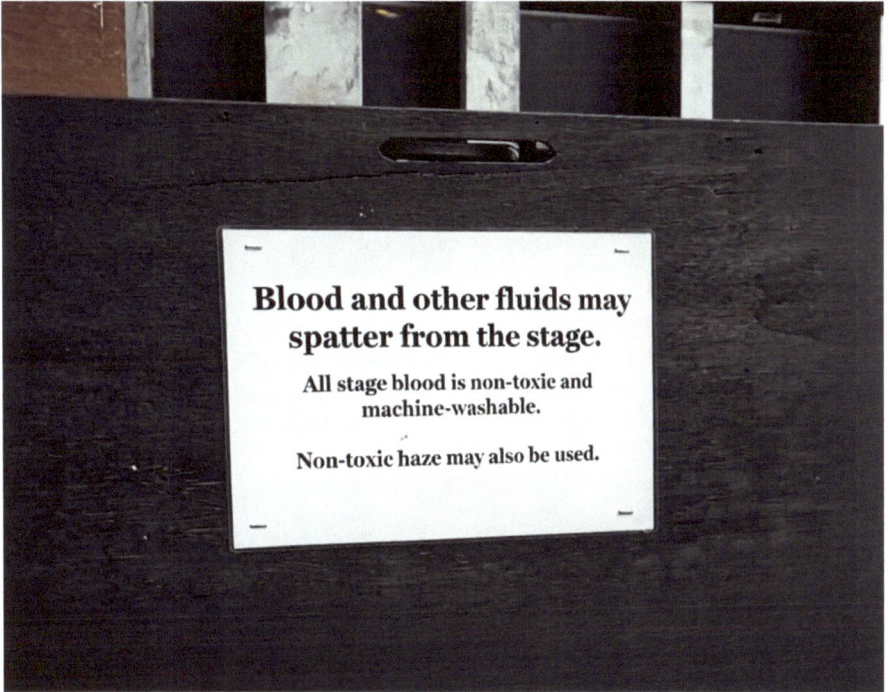

Top: One of the front of house warning signs at Pop-up Globe Auckland. Bottom: 'Other fluids' spatter from the stage as Sir Oliver Martext (Barry De Lore) vomits drunkenly into the yard, watchd by Duke Senior (Rawiri Paratene) and Duke Frederick (Stephen Butterworth) during As You Like It at Pop-up Globe Auckland, 2017. This moment always brought huge laughs and gasps.

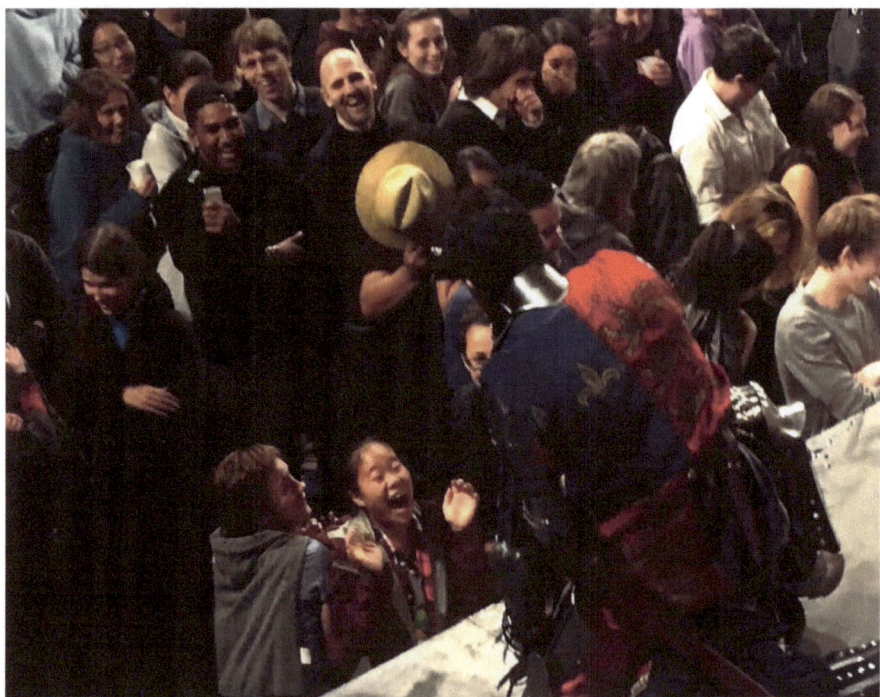

Top: Henry V (Chris Huntly-Turner) brutally cuts the throat of the Constable of France (Antonio Te Maioha), during Henry V at Pop-up Globe Auckland , 2017. Blood would sometimes spray up to six metres from the stage, to the delight of the audience. Bottom: A reverse shot of the same moment taken during a different performance shows the remarkable reactions of nearby audience members.

Top: Henry V (Chris Huntly-Turner) has just ordered the hanging of his old friend Bardolph (Adrian Hooke), in Henry V at Pop-up Globe Auckland, 2017. Bardolph was hoisted high in the air in this tragic yet spectacular moment. Bottom: Iago (Haakon Smested) hangs high above the stage, blood dripping from his corpse, at the conclusion of Othello, Pop-up Globe Auckland, 2017.

Dogberry (Kieran Mortell) abseils into the crowd at Pop-up Globe Melbourne, 2017, drawing gasps and cheers from the delighted audience who turn to watch him. These moments of spectacle bring immense energy to performances and are a key ingredient of Bloody Good Shakespeare.

Othello (Regan Taylor) chokes Iago (Haakon Smested) during Othello at Pop-up Globe Melbourne, 2017-18. Stage combat this close to an audience elicits unforgettable reactions.

Top: The playhouse is illuminated by spectacular red pyrotechnics at the conclusion of Othello, Pop-up Globe Auckland, 2017. Bottom: Horatio (Barry De Lore) is amazed by the ghostly flaming sword held by Hamlet (Adrian Hooke) at Pop-up Globe Perth, 2019.

Tears & Laughter

SHAKESPEARE'S GENIUS LIES IN his profound understanding of human experience, which is never wholly tragic nor wholly comic. Life doesn't split cleanly into categories. It swerves, surprises, confounds. His plays follow suit. The richest moments of theatre - both onstage and in the audience – arise when laughter and tears coexist, when the emotional spectrum is stretched to its extremes.

To stage Shakespeare's plays as exclusively 'sad' tragedies or 'funny' comedies is to fail. It is to dismiss their depth, their texture, their visceral hold on audiences. The plays work because they embrace the full spectrum of life's unpredictability.

Comedy and tragedy, then, are not opposites. They are entwined. They sharpen one another.

Shakespeare wasn't the first dramatist to blend tones, but he was the boldest and most influential. In ancient Greek theatre, tragedy and comedy were strictly divided – not just in tone, but in how and when they were performed. Tragedy was reserved for exploring fate, divine justice, and suffering; comedy was for satire and farce, performed at separate festivals with entirely different aims. Even in the work of Euripides, who dared to explore psychology and irony, the plays themselves remained tonally consistent. The idea of a single play veering between comedy and despair was, for the Greeks, inconceivable.

That division held sway for centuries. In seventeenth-century France, neo-classical critics codified the 'rules' of drama: unity of time, place, and tone. A tragedy must be noble, serious, and unbroken in its gravity. Comedy should remain light and separated from darker themes. Shakespeare's defiance of these rules was seen by some as genius, by others as an affront. Some saw a lack of discipline in the way his plays danced between modes. But others saw something radical and true – a theatre that echoed the shifting unpredictability of life itself.

In this, Shakespeare found few real precursors in English drama. Earlier playwrights, like John Heywood or the anonymous authors of morality plays, had used humour to make didactic points, but they did not approach the emotional complexity or tonal layering that Shakespeare mastered. Even the early tragedies and comedies of Marlowe and Kyd were largely unmixed in tone. It was Shakespeare who fully broke the barrier.

He understood something fundamental: emotion is not partitioned. We laugh before we cry. We cry and then laugh again. The tragic only cuts deep if it pierces through something light. The comic only truly lands if it dances near the edge of danger.

This fusion is a theatrical device of immense power. When an audience laughs, their emotional defences drop. That laughter becomes the gateway through which tragedy enters more deeply. Likewise, moments of levity in dark plays don't undercut the tragedy; they heighten it. The audience is jolted by the shift, and in that jolt, they *feel*.

This interplay of light and dark is a signature. It is Shakespeare's theatrical fingerprint.

And yet, even now, modern critics often prefer their genres neatly boxed. Tragedies should be sad. Comedies, funny. This critical expectation leads to misunderstanding Shakespeare's dramaturgy. Productions that smooth over the tonal complexities rob the audience of the emotional whiplash that makes these plays so immediate and affecting.

If we do not find these juxtapositions in Shakespeare's work, the fault is not in the text, but in its interpretation.

I've experienced this tension first-hand. At Pop-up Globe, our bold tonal shifts often drew fire. With my 2019 *Romeo and Juliet*, we chose to stage the first half as a full-blooded comedy. Audiences laughed hard – and then the mood shifted, fast and irrevocably. Critics were uneasy with this approach, suggesting it made the ending less tragic. But in performance, we saw the opposite. The laughter drew the audience close. It made the fall hurt more.

These choices are not always safe. But they are, I believe, true to Shakespeare. He was not writing tragedies and comedies. He was writing life. Our job is not to tidy that up. It is to stage it, in all its mess and magnificence.

Can one go too far? Of course. An overly broad comedic performance in the midst of a tragic arc can break the spell. A descent into relentless bleakness in a comedy drains it of vitality. The key is balance – a director must ride the rhythms of Shakespeare's text, understanding when to allow the audience release and when to hold them in unbearable tension. It is a mistake to assume that an audience should only feel one emotion at a time. Great theatre, like great life, allows for complexity.

Shakespeare's plays, when done right, feel like life itself – unpredictable, rich, and ever-shifting. They should never be locked into narrow emotional boxes. Bloody Good Shakespeare embraces the constant interplay of light and dark, of high and low. Laughter sharpens sorrow. Sorrow deepens laughter.

Tragedy

Tragedy is not sadness. Tragedy is life, rushing forward, ecstatic, irresistible – until suddenly it isn't. The mistake, the great mistake, is to play tragedy as though the ending is inevitable, as though the characters are already dead, their fates etched in stone before they have even begun. To play tragedy like this is to make it tedious, to leech it of its power, to forget that the heart of tragedy is not despair but loss. And loss is only powerful if there is something magnificent to lose.

Too often, Shakespearean tragedy is played like a funeral from the start. But this is not how life works. People fight for life, even keep a sense of humour, right to the end. Romeo himself alludes to it – the *lightning before death*. The best tragedies play for lightness as long as possible. This is not a trick, not a ploy to manipulate an audience. It is life itself. If you don't make 'em laugh in the first half, they won't cry in the second. And if they don't cry in the second, you've failed.

I have always believed that tragedy must be fought against. No one in a Shakespeare play thinks they are in a tragedy. Romeo never looks at Juliet and says, *How sad it is that we're doomed.* He says, *With love's light wings did I o'erperch these walls.* There is no doom in him. He is alive, utterly alive, and so is she. And that is why, when the tragedy comes, it hurts. Because we believed in their joy. Because we saw hope. Because, in their lightness, we came to love them. And then they died.

Decision moments: the crucible of tragedy

At the heart of every great tragedy lies not circumstance but choice. Too many productions of Shakespeare's tragedies treat the protagonists as victims of fate, swept along by forces beyond their control. This is a fundamental misunderstanding of how tragedy works. Tragedy is not about things happening to people; it is about people making choices, often impossible choices, and then facing the consequences.

Decision moments are what make tragedy tragic rather than merely sad. When Othello chooses to believe Iago, when Romeo chooses to drink the poison – these are not moments when fate crushes the character, but moments when the character makes a choice. And the audience must see the choice in all its terrible clarity, understand what the stakes are in the moment and why the choice is hard for the character. It is for the audience to consider the consequences of each choice, and to do this, the moment of the decision is paramount. The stakes must be high.

What are stakes? Simply put, they are what the character risks losing. Physical life, of course, but also love, honour, legacy, redemption, immortality. In Shakespeare, stakes are always both personal and cosmic. When Richard III seizes the throne, he is not merely risking personal power but the entire social and political order.

The director's task is to make these stakes real, to ensure the audience feels them viscerally. This is not done through explanation or exposition, but through staging that emphasises the personal cost, the human value, of what might be lost.

In my 2019 production of *Romeo and Juliet*, we established value early and clearly. The love between the young couple was radiant, transcendent, worth dying for. The friendship between Romeo, Benvolio and Mercutio was palpable, playful and funny. Only then would the loss of all this matter. This is why productions that rush to the tragedy, that treat the love story as a prelude to the real drama, always fail. The stakes were established in the laughter between the young male friends, at Capulet's joyful ball, in the balcony scene, in the tenderness of the morning parting, in the giddy plans for the future. When those were taken away, the audience felt bereft – not merely sad that people died, but devastated that this particular love had been extinguished, that these wonderful, funny, lively young people were dead.

In Ben Naylor's 2017 production of *Othello* at Pop-up Globe, the stakes were elevated through the genuine love between Othello and Desdemona. In the early scenes, he emphasised the joy of the marriage, the real connection between them. Their first entrance together was accompanied by music, by celebration, by humour. The audience saw them happy, saw what they had to lose. When Iago began his work, the contrast was sharper, the stakes higher. By the final scene, when Othello enters Desdemona's bedchamber, the audience was not resigned to the tragedy – they were fighting it, silently willing the characters to break free from their fate.

Props as symbols: the physical language of loss

Theatre is not cinema. It cannot rely on close-ups, on subtle changes of expression, on the intimate whisper. It must communicate through the body, through space, and through objects. In Shakespeare's tragedies, props become not merely practical tools but potent symbols, physical manifestations of power, love, life, and death.

The most powerful props in tragedy are often the simplest: a letter, a ring, a sword, a vial of poison. Their power lies not only in purposeful design but in how they are used, in the meaning with which they are invested. These moments of exchange, of transformation, of loss, speak more eloquently than pages of dialogue.

A well-chosen prop, handled with intention, becomes a repository of meaning. It carries the weight of the narrative, embodies the stakes, makes concrete what might otherwise remain abstract. In tragedy, props should never be mere decoration or historical detail. They must be charged with life and significance. Choose them wisely. Consider a prop's journey through the production as carefully as you would the journey of a character.

Born to trouble: villains who steal the play

Villains are the lifeblood of tragedy. A great villain is a presence so compelling that the audience wants to be on their side. Iago, Richard III, Lady Macbeth – they do not tell us that they are wicked. They seduce us. They invite us in. They charm. And because we go with them, because we allow ourselves to enjoy their intelligence, their wit, their dark delight, we feel the fall all the more keenly.

In Pop-up Globe's 2018 *Richard III*, we deliberately played against the stereotype of the hobbling villain. The brilliant comic actor Stephen Butterworth as Richard was charismatic, physically commanding despite his deformity, irresistibly funny. The audience laughed with him, became complicit in his schemes. When he suddenly turned on Hastings and had him executed – *Off with his head! Now, by Saint Paul I swear, / I will not dine until I see the same* – the sudden shift to violence was shocking precisely because the audience had previously been charmed by him. It landed because we had thoroughly enjoyed his ascent – and now found that the man we'd been cheering on was a sociopath.

The best villains first turn the audience into their allies, and then try to keep them as allies even as they descend into madness and destruction.

The balance of life and death

Shakespearean tragedy relies on movement, violence, dance, and spectacle. Fights must be real, not polite stage combat but messy, visceral, fast. The danger must feel present. And the moments of music, of song, of revelry, are the backbone of the experience. Shakespeare knew that music is the language of emotion, that it bypasses reason and goes straight to the heart. A song in the right place can transform a scene. Desdemona's *Willow Song* in *Othello* is not just an interlude; it is the sound of a woman fearing death.

Shakespearean tragedies are thrillers. They rush forward, they sweep the audience up in their momentum, and only at the very end, only when it is too late, do they let us see the full weight of what has been lost. In rehearsal, guard against the gift of seeing the future. Remind your actors that their characters do not know what will happen in the future. They generally make choices that seem right at the time, just like the rest of us. The tragedy lies in their discovery that their well-intentioned choices have led them to unexpected, unforeseen death.

A production must never be staged for the pleasure of those who already know the play inside out, even though we know there will normally be some in the audience who do. It must be made for those who are seeing it for the first time, who do not know what happens next, who do not know that Hamlet will die, that Lear will hold Cordelia in his arms, that Romeo will drink the poison.

And tragedy always involves death. Shakespeare's comedies start with chaos and end with order (almost always with marriage, that great symbol of order in Shakespeare's world), and his tragedies start with order and end with the chaos of blood and untimely mortality.

Tragedy exists to remind us what matters. To show us joy, and then to take it away. To make us laugh, and then to break our hearts as the bright blood sprays. Shakespeare understood this balance better than anyone. His tragedies contain some of the greatest humour ever written because contrast amplifies impact. Without light, there can be no darkness. Without moments of levity, sorrow becomes one-note, monotonous, and ineffective.

And even in the wreckage – even in the final moments of a tragedy – the final image must be life. The curtain call is the moment when the play turns to the audience and says, *You have felt this. You have watched us die. Now go back into the world, and live.* This is not a dismissal of tragedy's emotional force but a recognition of its function: not to mire us in sorrow, but to reinvigorate our appreciation of life. The catharsis of tragedy should not leave the audience numb but awaken something within them, a renewed sense of what it means to love, to lose, and to endure.

Comedy

Comedy lives, it breathes, it dies if left unattended. Shakespeare understood this. His comedies are built on action – on the unexpected, on disruption, on sudden shifts of power. But they are difficult, potentially much more challenging to successfully stage than the tragedies.

People laugh when they understand what is happening, moment by moment. But Shakespeare is clever – his comedy makes the audience feel smart, only to expose their own foolishness. The trick is in the fall – the pompous man undone, the wise fool victorious.

Laughter is release. Shakespeare knew that. He plants comedy in the heart of tension, lets the audience gasp, then hugs them with laughter. It isn't a break from the play – it's the play itself. The Porter in *Macbeth* follows bloodshed. Shakespeare means the Porter to be comic. The script is clear. Trust Shakespeare by ensuring the audience laughs at the Porter, by any means necessary. His jokes must be funny, because they are relief from the horror. They must be funny, to make the horror that will follow even more intense.

Shakespeare's comedies mock systems, unravel authority, expose hypocrisy. They lure the audience in with laughter, then twist the knife. *Measure for Measure* is full of comedy – cheek by jowl with dark, uncomfortable, danger-ous events and characters. Our production leaned into that, using laughter to pull the audience deeper into the unease. The more they realised they shouldn't laugh, the more they did.

Comedy is exact. Each beat is critical. Great comedy is repeatable – it should always get a laugh (or at least a smile), the beats should generally be the same every time. Ensure every moment is precise, every reaction calculated to take the audience to places they didn't expect. We introduced modern pop songs played on old instruments, placed modern props in the hands of characters in perfect Jacobean period dress, creating visual incongruities that disrupted expectations and sharpened the absurdity. Laughs must be earned through precision, never left to chance.

The eleven commandments of Shakespearean comedy

1. Clowns & fools aren't funny (by themselves)

The greatest mistake a director can make is assuming that clowns and fools generate laughter simply by existing. They don't. They are only funny in relation to the world around them. Their role is not to amuse in isolation, but to expose absurdity, deflate pomposity, and make those in power look ridicu-lous. The best Shakespearean comic roles, from fools like Feste to clowns like Touchstone, wield their wit like weapons, puncturing the delusions of the high-status characters they encounter.

Fools are the audience on stage, seeing the play with the audience's eyes, able to influence the play on the audience's behalf. Clowns are rock stars, and they must bring rockstar energy. If you're not sure what that looks like, check out the image of Michael Mahoney as Touchstone in Tom Mallburn's Pop-up Globe production of *As You Like It* at the end of this chapter. As the crowd roars he stands, arms outstretched, mandolin at his waist, at the conclusion of one of his many songs. That's what I'm talking about. Look for clowns and fools who can sing, play instruments, dance. Seek to bring all of their talents onto the stage.

I think that playing clowns with absolute sincerity – never reaching for a laugh, never playing for the joke – makes them funnier. Their comedy lies in their truthfulness. The audience laughs because the clown is speaking a reality no one else dares to voice. This requires exceptional timing and an awareness of the audience's reactions. A successful clown knows that stillness can be just as powerful as movement, that a well-placed glance can land harder than a shouted punchline. A misstep, a misjudged pause, or a moment of indulgence can kill the momentum entirely. Comedy may look like chaos, but it's emphatically not; it's control disguised as spontaneity. Clowns must exist in a world that believes itself serious, undermining it from within.

Be under no illusions: Clowns and fools are the most difficult parts to master. Look for that rockstar energy and create a space for it to explode.

2. Every beat matters

Great comedy is a science. Every pause, every glance, every shift in tone is a calculation. Drill comic routines endlessly, refining the sequence of beats until they are razor-sharp. Comedy thrives on rhythm – too slow, and the energy dies; too fast, and the audience doesn't have time to process the turn. There is no space for approximation. Precision is everything.

This is why at Pop-up Globe we studied the architecture of laughter, breaking it down into its mechanics – pace, timing, escalation, contrast. We stripped routines down to their bones and rebuilt them, shaping each performance into something that felt fresh but was, in reality, meticulously crafted. A successful comedic sequence should function like a piece of music, with crescendos and rests, syncopation and surprise.

One of the best examples for me is the 'box hedge' scene from *Twelfth Night*. Three low characters, hidden 'in the box hedge' observe a fourth, high status character, Malvolio, as he reads a fake letter that gives him hopes far above his station. Instead of a single hedge, though, we introduced three individual hedges. These could roll about the stage. Choreographing this complex scene was extremely difficult, but paid off hugely in performance. Comedy must always feel like it is expanding, that the audience never know what could come next.

Rehearsing comedy means testing every option. Would this line be funnier if it were delayed? Should this movement be sudden or gradual? Should the laugh come from the situation, the reaction, or the juxtaposition of the two? Each choice builds on the next, leading to a well-calibrated explosion of laughter. When we introduced props, we treated them as instruments – extensions of the character's comic vocabulary. A hat placed at the wrong moment, a cup dropped just slightly too late, a trip and a fall through an open trapdoor – each detail makes the difference between a mild chuckle and a belly laugh.

Drill not just for clarity but for consistency. The joke, the routine, the business must land every single time. It is this repetition, the ability to make the audience feel that what they are seeing is spontaneous even though it has been precisely tuned, that defines true comedic craftsmanship. It is not enough to get a laugh once.

3. Surprise is the heart of laughter

A joke is an ambush. The audience expects one thing, and suddenly, they get another. That sharp left turn – the unexpected shift, the jolt of absurdity – is where laughter lives. Shakespeare understood this deeply. His plays are filled with reversals, misunderstandings, and sudden bursts of chaos. But surprise must be genuine.

We created moments of unpredictability – not just in the text, but in the staging. A Porter in *Macbeth* that undid his trousers, pulled out a realistic looking penis, and urinated on the groundlings. Cutting the throat of a Syracusan prisoner at the start of *The Comedy of Errors*, using a blood pump so that bright arterial blood sprayed up to the second story. These surprises aren't random, and they are not necessarily *funny*, either; they are designed to heighten the experience of the performance.

The best comedic actors understand how to play against expectations. If an audience is prepared for a joke, they must be led somewhere else first, so the laugh is never given cheaply. The moment an audience believes they know what's coming, comedy dies. We worked to keep them on edge, to make every discovery feel spontaneous, even though it had been rigorously rehearsed.

A well-timed surprise can elevate a joke from amusing to unforgettable. Take Malvolio's yellow stockings in *Twelfth Night*. The laugh isn't just in the stockings themselves; it's in the shock of the other characters, in their rapid, awful realisation of how foolish he looks, in Malvolio's own obliviousness to the absurdity. This only works if he looks palpably, obviously ridiculous – yet it must still be conceivable that the character made these choices seriously, not for comic intent. These big set piece moments are critical and must be exploited ruthlessly for comic advantage.

Surprise is recognition and comprehension. The best moments of Shakespearean comedy make the audience see something familiar in a completely new, understandable way. That is the joy of laughter – the sudden, exhilarating collision of the expected and the unexpected, the moment where sense and nonsense briefly trade places, taking the audience along for the ride.

4. Laughter is a collaboration

Comedy is a conversation. The audience are essential participants, and their laughter shapes the landscape of the performance. A well-timed pause, a knowing glance, a direct address to a spectator – these moments create an intimacy that elevates the humour beyond mere performance into an experience shared between actor and audience. At Pop-up Globe we trained actors to listen to the crowd, to anticipate where laughter would fall, and to adjust accordingly. If a joke landed harder than expected, we allowed space for the laughter to breathe. If a moment didn't get the response we anticipated, we adjusted our pacing and delivery on the fly. Comedy must be reactive.

Working with the audience means understanding that no two performances are identical. Different crowds respond to different things. A matinee audience of schoolchildren will laugh at different beats than an evening crowd of seasoned theatre-goers. Make it a rule to always watch the audience, to sense their mood and adapt. Some nights, a pause held a second longer will make a joke explode. Other nights, a line that normally brought a roar will need an extra glance, a slight gesture, to land. The ability to pivot mid-performance, to let the audience guide the energy, is a skill actors must hone obsessively. True comedy happens in the moment.

5. Ensemble: a machine for comedy

A great ensemble is a living, breathing comic machine. Comedy goes far beyond the leading roles – it thrives in the interactions between the entire cast. The best Shakespearean comedies capitalise on the power of the group, from the bumbling chaos of *A Midsummer Night's Dream*'s mechanicals to the individual soldiers of *Henry V*.

Ensure that every character has a purpose, that every reaction adds to the comedic energy. Give minor characters unexpected asides or planned 'ad-libs', moments of business that undercut the pomp of main players, subtle (or sometimes not-so-subtle) movements that amplify the humour. The result? A comedy that will feel alive – a world in which everyone, not just the leads, contributes to the laughter. There's a great image of the ensemble in *The Comedy Of Errors* at the end of this chapter that shows this in action. Led by Stephen Lovatt as Dr Pinch, the disguised ensemble has become a living comedy organism that interacts with the undisguised leads to create a world of mayhem and surprise.

6. Low comedy has a place – and it must earn it

Shakespeare knew that comedy exists on a spectrum, from the witty word-play of Beatrice and Benedick to the outright buffoonery of Dogberry. Slap-stick, bodily functions, drunken antics – low comedy has always had a place on the stage, but it must be used with precision. Don't be afraid to use these tools – vomiting, pratfalls, characters tripping over their own arrogance – but ensure they always serve the moment. A perfectly timed piece of physical comedy can enhance a scene, but indulgence or overuse can drag it down. We made sure to test everything: If a sequence got laughs, we kept it. If it didn't, it was cut.

Low comedy works best when it punctuates moments of higher tension. A sudden pratfall after a deeply serious monologue can be devastatingly funny.

We choreographed our slapstick with the same rigour as a fight sequence – every fall, every slap, every stumble was carefully plotted. The trick is commitment: an actor must perform these moments with total sincerity. If a fall looks deliberate, it loses its effect. But if a character appears genuinely oblivious to their own ridiculousness, the laughter erupts.

7. Making old jokes land

Shakespeare's words are brilliant – but humour is rooted in context. What was blisteringly funny to an Elizabethan audience may now pass unnoticed, or worse, create confusion. That doesn't mean the joke should be abandoned. It means it needs translation.

If a line is clearly meant to be funny, and it's met with silence, the problem is not the audience – it's the moment. And it's our responsibility as directors to make that moment work.

Sometimes, that means changing a word or two. In 3.ii of *Twelfth Night*, Sir Andrew Aguecheek expresses his disdain for political cunning by declaring, *An't be any way, it must be with valour; for policy I hate: I had as lief be a Brownist as a politician.* This reference to the Brownists – a puritan religious sect that barely registers today – became 'estate agents' in our production. The joke landed. Every night. The laughter was about recognition. We didn't change the scene's meaning, just the access point.

Other times, the entire moment may need to go. When the audience has no hope of comprehending a section – when it's dense, archaic, and irrelevant – cut it. Holofernes in *Love's Labour's Lost* is a good example. There are versions of that character that work, but when the language becomes so impenetrable that even a skilled actor can't bring it to life, it's time to reassess.

Physicality can help bridge the gap. A single look, a knowing gesture, a contemporary beat inserted into a Renaissance frame – these can spark laughter without a single line changed. We had a moment in *Henry V* where the Dauphin's deliberately rude gift of a box of tennis balls included a hidden wooden hand that flipped the middle finger as the lid lifted. It was silly. It was completely untextual. And it brought the house down. Because it was right for that moment. Because it served and expanded the story.

The guiding principle is simple: comedy must be immediate. If a joke falls flat, fix it. If the audience doesn't laugh, rework it. Not because Shakespeare needs improving, but because his work was never static to begin with. He was writing for a live audience in a living theatre. So must we.

Small, thoughtful tweaks. Bold, strategic cuts. Moments of modern connection nestled inside historical architecture. Acts of faith in Shakespeare's original mission: to connect, to provoke, to entertain. If the laughter isn't coming, the answer isn't to blame the audience. It's to meet them where they are – and bring Shakespeare to life in the now.

8. Milk the entrance/exit

Some of the greatest comic moments in Shakespearean performance come from the physical and visual setup of an entrance or exit . The key to making these hilarious is contrast – the higher the character's status, the more ridiculous the situation must be. Shakespeare understood this perfectly.

To make an entrance land, two elements must be considered. The scene that the character enters into, and how the character responds to it. Consider a set up where several on-stage characters have quite logically arrived at searching for a missing ring in each other's clothing. It is perfectly innocent. But when another character enters, the on-stage action is revealed as a tableau without – for the entering character – any explanation of the events that led up to it. This is classic comedy. The next element is how the arriving character responds to what they are seeing. Are they shocked? Or delighted? The two beats must be timed perfectly.

At Pop-up Globe, we drilled these moments with a ruthless attention to timing. Too fast, and the moment is lost. Too slow, and the audience has time to anticipate the reveal. But when executed perfectly, with a doubletake from the stage to the audience, the result is a gasp then an eruption of laughter. Every entrance is an opportunity for comedy – if exploited with precision.

Exits have their own rhythm. Disrupting this – in service of the story – is the key to finding humour. Let's say we have a high-status character who is too haughty, too arrogant, and needs knocking down a peg or two. Mid-scene, the high-status character moves to exit, having a delivered a killer line to the other on-stage characters. She finds the door is locked unexpectedly. She rattles it. Nothing. Then she has to acknowledge to the other characters that there is a problem. She knocks on the door. There is an uncomfortable pause. Everyone has to wait. The door is opened by a servant figure. The servant has an attitude. The high status character finally exits past the servant. The servant gives everyone left on stage a dirty look, and closes the door.

Here comedy has served our story. Even the high-status character can't magic a door open. She has to rely on being helped sometimes. And it's clearly difficult for her to get good staff these days. But the servant is loyal – suggesting deeper relationships in the household than might otherwise be apparent.

9. Escalate relentlessly

Repetition is one of the oldest tools in comedy, and Shakespeare wielded it brilliantly. A joke that is funny once becomes funnier when it returns in an unexpected way. Study the structure of recurring jokes – whether it is a character misunderstanding the same word throughout a play, or a bit of physical business that escalates with each repetition. A gag repeated three times, each time building in absurdity, turns a mild chuckle into uncontrollable laughter.

The key to making repetition work is escalation and context. The second occurrence must be bigger than the first, in a new and less appropriate context, and the third must take it to an extreme. We experimented with running gags across entire productions. A seemingly incidental joke in the first few scenes would return in later scenes with an entirely different context, magnified in a way that took the audience by surprise or subverted their expectations. Ultimately, 'jokes' can even turn very serious and heighten tragedy.

1. First instance: Establish the joke in a straightforward context. *On leaving London, the Boy in* Henry V *is given a present by Mistress Quickly – a frying pan. He's not sure what to do with it.*

2. Second instance: Repeat in a heightened context with raised stakes. *At the seige of Harfleur, Henry's army, gathered in the yard amongst the audience, charge the stage. The penultimate figure is the Boy, wielding the frying pan. It's a joke, but it's also serious – he doesn't have any other weapon, and he's brave enough to fight the French with whatever he has to hand.*

3. Third instance: Maximum escalation in the most inappropriate context. Be brave. *During the battle of Agincourt, in the midst of a*

genuine and serious battle scene, the Boy is cornered by the Dauphin of France. Weaponless, he hits the Dauphin over the head with the frying pan. Cue laughter. The comedy is heightened by the serious context.

4. Optional callback: A final reference that continues or subverts the established joke. *At the end of the battle, news comes that the French have attacked the boys and the baggage train. A distraught Pistol brings on the bloody body of the Boy. King Henry walks over and picks up the frying pan, now battered and bloody. He looks at it – and holds it up to the audience for them to see. The joke is a joke no more. It's become a moving symbol of the Boy's courage, innocence, and the brutal cost of war. What started as a bit of comic business has turned into something else entirely – an object that now holds the weight of the story, a silent testament to the lives lost and the absurd, tragic heroism of battle.*

10. Silence is deadly (and hilarious)

Great comedy isn't just about the words – it's about *when* those words are spoken. It's a truism that timing is everything, and sometimes, the funniest thing an actor can do is nothing at all. A perfectly placed silence, a pause just long enough to let an idea sink in, can create laughter as powerful as the sharpest punchline.

Treat pauses as meticulously as you treat dialogue. The moment of realisation before a character recognises their mistake. The long, painful silence before a character reacts to an absurd statement. The unbearable tension before an awkward situation explodes into chaos. These pauses aren't accidental – they must be calculated, rehearsed, and polished until they feel utterly spontaneous.

Actors must listen, not just to each other, but to the audience. If a laugh is still rolling, the next line must wait. If a moment needs room to breathe, the actor must hold it. The comic pause is about control – knowing exactly when to let the silence stretch just a second longer than expected, before shattering it with the next move. It is the difference between a good performance and an unforgettable one.

Pauses can be used to build tension as well as release it. A silence held just slightly longer than expected can make the audience squirm in anticipation, making the eventual payoff even funnier. Play with using these gaps to shift the audience's focus, directing their attention toward an actor who remains motionless or to a prop left hanging in midair. Sometimes the mere act of waiting, of forcing the audience to lean forward, creates its own kind of hilarious agony. A comic pause is an unspoken contract with the audience, a setup for the perfect explosion of laughter. Use this sparingly, and wisely.

11. Disguises are a golden opportunity

Disguises in Shakespeare's plays are never just about deception – they are about transformation, revelation, and absurdity. They allow characters to navigate forbidden spaces, invert social hierarchies, and, most importantly, create moments of high comedy. The simple act of concealment leads to misunderstanding, mistaken identity, and the kind of surprise that makes an audience erupt in laughter. When wielded correctly, disguises turn the ordinary into the extraordinary and expose the absurdity hiding in plain sight.

Push disguises to their comic extreme. In *Twelfth Night*, Antonio – the burly sea captain – disguises himself to pursue Sebastian to Illyria. We decided to have him attempt to disguise as a woman – but as a sea-captain of limited means, his disguise would be home-made and poorly executed, complete with large balloons under his dress to serve as breasts. The audience was already laughing at the incongruity of the rugged Antonio attempting to pass unnoticed, but we didn't stop there. When the guards recognised him in Illyria, their shock and confusion heightened the moment. One guard, in disbelief, reached out to touch Antonio's 'breast' – which popped, thanks to a secret pin taped to the guard's finger. The effect was electric. The audience roared with laughter, not only because of the surprise and absurdity but because it fitted perfectly within the play's themes of disguise, cross-dressing, and mistaken identity.

This moment exemplified why disguises are such a powerful comedic tool in Shakespeare's plays. They are a source of theatrical delight. A well-executed disguise scene layers tension with comedy, leading the audience toward inevitable revelation but keeping them off balance until the perfect moment. Disguises invite boldness. They require actors to fully commit to the pretence while simultaneously signalling to the audience that they are in on the joke. The best disguises are those that heighten contrast: a nobleman reduced to servitude, a fierce warrior in an ill-fitting gown, a woman dressed as a man who is then mistaken for a woman again. Shakespeare's disguises are mechanisms of chaos, engines of irony, and, above all, golden opportunities for comedy.

To stage disguises effectively, a director must exploit every possibility for comedic escalation. Costumes might hinder movement, props can amplify the absurdity, and actors must embrace the serious/ridiculous. If an audience believes for even a second that the disguise is convincing - i.e. they cannot tell that the character is disguised and therefore become confused – the joke is lost. The humour lives in the disconnect – between who the character is and who they are pretending to be, between the world's acceptance of the disguise and the audience's disbelief. When done well, these moments transcend mere deception and become some of the most riotous, unforgettable sequences in all of Shakespearean theatre.

Reigniting the flame

Shakespeare's plays are rowdy, dangerous, and subversive. They are full of contradictions – laughter and sorrow, order and chaos, beauty and brutality – all jostling for space in the same breath.

Comedy is not confined to the comedies. It explodes through the histories and tragedies too. Shakespeare's comedies build to a fever pitch in the second half, where confusion, disguise, and desire reach their peak before collapsing into joyful resolution. His tragedies, meanwhile, are built on a foundation of joy. They begin with hope, with love, with laughter. The fall is only devastating because we believed so fully in what came before. Strip away that levity and you flatten the fall. You lose the reason we care.

And the histories – those so often misclassified as 'neither here nor there' – are perhaps the most excitingly blended of all. Here, Shakespeare moves freely between tavern and throne room, between Falstaff's low humour and Henry's battlefield rhetoric. The histories teach us that human drama is political, personal, and profoundly unpredictable. Their tonal variety isn't messy. It's masterful.

To direct Shakespeare is to embrace this tonal range. Every creative decision should be governed by a simple, ruthless logic: does it work? Does it make them laugh? Does it make them weep? Does it make them feel? If not – cut it, change it, try again. This is about showing respect for a playwright who understood life in all its complexity, who refused to fit it into neat categories, and who dared to write theatre that mirrored the full range of human experience.

The moment we flatten these peaks and troughs in order to 'play it safe', everyone loses.

Top: Touchstone (Michael Mahoney) shows the 'rock-star' energy demanded of Shakespeare's clowns during a performance of As You Like It *at Pop-up Globe Auckland, 2017. The moment is captured at the conclusion of one of his songs. Bottom: Dr Pinch (Stephen Lovatt) leads the disguised comic ensemble during a performance of* The Comedy Of Errors *at Pop-up Globe Auckland, 2018.*

Top: Juliet (Jess Hong) stabs herself over the body of Romeo (Darcy Kent) at Pop-up Globe Auckland, 2019-20. Blood flows over her fingers. The silence in the playhouse at these moments was palpable. Bottom: Macbeth (Stephen Lovatt), smeared with blood, engages Macduff (Matu Ngaropo) in a fight to the death at Pop-up Globe Auckland, 2018.

Top: Hecate (Clementine Mills) having magically appeared in a steaming cauldron, entrances Macbeth (Stephen Lovatt) at Pop-up Globe Sydney, 2018. Bottom: Stephen Lovatt (Macbeth), sits at the rear of the playhouse in a quiet moment during a performance. Playing lead roles in such physcial and demanding productions requires huge energy and concentration from actors.

Top: Alex Holloway directs Rebecca Rogers (Hermia), Harry Bradley (Lysander) and Simon Rodda (Demetrius) in a complex physical comedy sequence during rehearsals at Pop-up Globe Perth, 2019. Bottom: Hymen (John Bayne) descends from the heavens in the final scene of As You Like It at Pop-up Globe Auckland, 2017. Comedies must continually expand their boundaries through the show.

Theatre of Fire: A Manifesto

In this end is your beginning.

Shakespeare is waiting to be reignited. His words lie dormant on the page, ready to burst into flame at the touch of the right spark. And you, reading these words now, you are that spark. You are the one who can set this theatre ablaze again.

For too long, we have treated Shakespeare like a precious artefact, something to be handled with gloves, kept behind velvet ropes, admired from a distance. We have forgotten what he truly is: a living weapon, a wild force, a thunderstorm contained in verse. His theatre is dangerous, electric, immediate. It is meant to make the blood race and the heart pound. It is meant to leave an audience transformed.

At Pop-up Globe, we witnessed this transformation. Night after night, performance after performance, we saw it happen. The wonder in the eyes of groundlings as they felt the spray of stage blood across their faces for the first time. The roar of laughter that shook the steel beams above our heads. The collective gasp as a villain revealed himself, making direct eye contact with the crowd, turning them into conspirators. The profound silence that fell in the final moments of tragedy, eight hundred breaths held at once.

Modern Shakespearean theatre has lost its way. It has become too cerebral, too self-conscious, too afraid of its own power. It whispers when it should shout. It tiptoes when it should dance. It holds back when it should surge forward. Shakespeare knew better. He knew that theatre must engage the whole person: mind, heart, gut, groin. He knew that an audience want to be shaken. They want to be moved. They want to participate in telling the story.

So make theatre that includes your audience as storytelling collaborators. Make theatre that connects. Make theatre that sweats and bleeds and laughs and weeps. Do not settle for productions that are merely intellectual, merely tasteful, merely correct. Reach for something greater.

Find new spaces for your work. The performance space is an element that will colour all subsequent choices – and even govern the ultimate success of your production. If you must use a proscenium stage, light the audience as well, and find every possible opportunity to use all of the space for performance, bursting off the stage. But even stronger is to find a remarkable non-conventional space for the show. Become an explorer, and pioneer new spaces and new ways to stage these ancient plays.

Trust the actor. The actor is the living heart of Shakespeare's work. When you place the actor at the centre, when you let them connect directly with the audience, when you train them to share with clarity, with passion, with the full force of their humanity, then Shakespeare comes alive. An actor who brings inventiveness and joy, who knows how to connect with the audience, to use the verse, who understands the rhythm, who feels the pulse of the language in their body, is worth more than any elaborate staging or clever concept.

Tear down the wall. The fourth wall is a modern invention, a barrier that separates actor from audience, that treats spectators as voyeurs rather than participants. Shakespeare never knew such a wall. His theatre was an arena of shared light, shared space, shared breath. The actor spoke to the audience, looked them in the eye, made them complicit in the action. This is the foundation of theatrical power. When you address the audience directly, when you acknowledge their presence, when you make them part of the story, you create an experience that cannot be replicated in any other medium. Human connection is the beating heart of live performance.

Embrace the body. Shakespeare's theatre was physical. It was sweaty. It was visceral. It was dangerous. Fights were explosive bursts of violence that made the audience fear for the actor's safety. Blood flowed. Bodies fell. The stage itself became a battlefield, a bedroom, a throne room, a forest, a storm-tossed ship. All through the power of the actor's body, the actor's voice, the actor's belief.

Find comedy in tragedy. Find darkness in comedy. Shakespeare knew that life contains both, often in the same moment. His tragedies are filled with jokes, with clowns, with moments of absurd humour that make the darkness that follows even more devastating. His comedies contain shadows, threats, moments of genuine danger that make the laughter that follows even more liberating. This balance is what makes his work so profoundly human. If you play *Macbeth* without laughter, you diminish it. If you play *Twelfth Night* without cruelty, you trivialise it. The mixture is the magic.

Move fast. Shakespeare's plays were performed without intervals, without elaborate scene changes, without blackouts or pauses. The action flowed from one scene to the next with relentless momentum. You should do the same. Keep the energy high. Keep the pace brisk. Don't let the audience settle back in their seats. Don't give them time to disengage. Pull them forward. Make them hungry for what comes next.

Make it spectacular. A thunderous drumbeat that shakes the floor. A dance that transforms the entire stage. The spray of blood from a fresh wound. The terrible beauty of a stage filled with bodies after the final battle. Flaming torches, flaming arrows, flaming swords, smoke, pyrotechnics, firing cannons, a sea of bubbles filling the whole volume of the theatre. These moments of pure delight are what audiences remember. These are the images that burn themselves into the brain, that haunt the imagination long after the play has ended.

Above all, make it necessary. In an age of endless digital distraction, of content that can be paused, skipped, consumed at convenience, live theatre must justify its existence, must own itself. It must offer something that cannot be found elsewhere. It must be an event, a full evening's experience, not merely a performance. It must feel as though it is happening for the first time, right now, in this space, with these people.

The world does not need more polite, reverent, bloodless Shakespeare. It does not need more conceptual frameworks, more academic approaches, more productions that treat the text as a problem to be solved rather than a fire to be lit.

I have seen what Shakespeare can be when it is set free. I have stood in Pop-up Globe's 'steel O' and felt the air crackle with the energy of eight hundred people experiencing something primal, something necessary, something that connected them not just to each other but to generations of theatregoers stretching back four centuries.

I have seen actors transformed by the power of direct address, by the freedom to speak without microphones, by the challenge of holding a crowd with nothing but their voice, their body, and their belief. I have seen audiences weep, shout with laughter, gasp in horror, sit in stunned silence.

I have heard the applause fade as the company leaves the stage to be replaced by a babble and chatter of excitement, of the thrill of having collectively witnessed a kind of miracle. I have seen Shakespeare work as it was meant to work: as an event, as a communion, as a revolution.

The challenge before you is clear: Will you make theatre that confirms what people already believe, or will you make theatre that changes how they see the world? Will you offer comfort, or will you offer transformation? Will you preserve Shakespeare behind a glass fourth wall, or will you set him loose among us?

This is your revolution now. This is your moment to reclaim the radical spirit of a playwright who wrote for everyone, from groundlings to royalty. This is your chance to reconnect with a theatrical tradition that saw no distinction between high art and entertainment.

Take what you've learned in these pages. Take the principles, the practices, the provocations. Make them yours. Push them further than I ever could. Find the fire at the heart of Shakespeare and let it burn through everything you do.

The work will not be easy. Nothing worth doing ever is. You will face resistance. You will face ridicule and snide criticism from those who have never made anything of any real worth themselves. You will face the weight of tradition, the inertia of expectation, the fear of failure.

But you will also discover something extraordinary: the sheer, undeniable power of Shakespeare when he is allowed to be himself. Not 'great literature'. A living, breathing, dangerous playwright whose work will shake us to our core.

This is your time. The space is empty. The stage is bare. The audience is waiting.

Step forward. Take a breath.

It's time to make Bloody Good Shakespeare.

Acknowledgements

He aha te mea nui? Māku e kii atu, he tāngata, he tāngata, he tāngata.
What is the most important thing in the world? Well, let me tell you, it is
people, it is people, it is people.

– Whakataukī (Māori proverb)

I wish to express my heartfelt thanks to Ngāti Whātua Ōrākei, mana whenua of Tāmaki Makaurau, for their blessings and support of our Pop-up Globes in Aotearoa New Zealand.

There are, of course, far too many people to thank here for their help, guidance, fellowship, and collaboration at Pop-up Globe and beyond, but here are some who stand out particularly in my memory: Tim Fitzpatrick and Russell Emerson of Sydney University; Tobias Grant; Pop-up Globe's General Manager Anne Barrowclough; Ray Kingston who served as Chairman of our Board for the first vital years; Kelly Gilbride, Alice Pearce, Susan Earle, Ella Julienne and Tessa Mitchelson; my fellow stage directors Eddie Bijl, Ben Naylor, David Lawrence, Miriama McDowell, Tom Mallaburn, and Rita Stone; Head of Costume Design Bob Capocci and Head of Wardrobe Chantelle Gerrard; Composer Paul McLaney; Head of Stage Combat & Special Effects Alexander Holloway; Head of Scenic Design Malcolm Dale, John and Al Charles, and their colleagues; Movement Director Brigid Costello and others; Playhouse Manager Kevin Hill, FOH Managers Danny and Kim, and our Front of House teams, especially our dozens of volunteer ushers; Oscar West and dozens of musicians; the wardrobe department and dressers; our stage managers, particularly Bubbles, Liam, Chanelle and Jono; photographers Peter Meecham and Timothy Jules Hull; over 250 actors from many different countries; and, most importantly, our audiences.

A special mention to: Peter Thomson, Lesley Wade Soule and Chris Mc-Cullough at Exeter University; Martin White and Sara-Jane Bailes at Bristol University; my former colleagues and friends at British Touring Shakespeare, especially Dom Jinks; Maurice Ward and the board and staff of the Maltings Theatre Trust; The Durham Revue of 1999 who shaped my understanding of theatre and comedy so much and remain my good friends; our brilliant company lawyer Chris Hoquard of Dominion Law; Dr. Nick Brown; Tim & Kate Hall; Theo Bosanquet; former Mayor of Auckland Len Brown; Barbara Holloway and her colleagues at Auckland City Council and Auckland Tourism, Events and Economic Development; Sandra Roberts; Luke Hede and his team at Live Nation Australia; John Taylor; John Cox; Jeremy Fleming and his team at Stagekings; the team at Ellerslie Racecourse; and Steve Walker of King's College Auckland who is both a brilliant educator and a true Shakespearean.

My warm thanks to my proof-readers, particularly Rob Webb and my very patient family. Any errors that remain are naturally mine alone.

Photographic Credits

Some images are reproduced from Wikimedia Commons and used under the Creative Commons Attribution-Share Alike 4.0 International Licence (CC BY-SA 4.0), https://creativecommons.org/licenses/by-sa/4.0/

Some images are reproduced under fair dealing provisions for the purposes of criticism, commentary, and education. All images are credited. No endorsement by the rights holders is implied.

P.4-5 – Pop-up Globe Auckland at Ellerslie, 2017. Photo by Miles Gregory, © 2017.

P.24-25 – Interior of Pop-up Globe Auckland during a performance of Much Ado About Nothing (Dir: Miriama McDowell), Auckland 2017. Photo by Peter Meecham, Wikimedia Commons, CC BY-SA 4.0.

P.43 – TOP & BOTTOM: Photo by Miles Gregory, © 2019.

P.44 – Photo by Miles Gregory, © 2019.

P.60 – TOP: Henry V embraces an audience member in Henry V (Dir. Miles Gregory), Auckland 2017. Photo by Peter Meecham, © Pop-up Globe Inter-

national Ltd 2017. Used under fair dealing for educational commentary and critical analysis. BOTTOM: Dogberry shakes hands with an audience member in Much Ado About Nothing (Dir. Miriam McDowell), Auckland 2017. Photo by Peter Meecham, © Pop-up Globe International Ltd 2017. Used under fair dealing for educational commentary and critical analysis.

P.61 – TOP: Photo by Miles Gregory, © 2020. BOTTOM: Photo by Miles Gregory, © 2017.

P.62 – TOP: Photo by Benny Vandergast, Wikimedia Commons, CC BY-SA 4.0. BOTTOM: Photo by Benny Vandergast, Wikimedia Commons, CC BY-SA 4.0.

P.73 – Photo by Miles Gregory, © 2019.

P.74 – TOP: Photo by Miles Gregory, © 2018. BOTTOM: Photo by Miles Gregory, © 2019.

P.95 – TOP: Photo by Miles Gregory, © 2015. BOTTOM: Photo by Miles Gregory, © 2017.

P.96 – TOP: Photo by Timothy Jules Hull | www.globaltimoto.com, © 2017. BOTTOM: Photo by Miles Gregory, © 2019.

P.97 – TOP: Photo by Miles Gregory, © 2019. BOTTOM: Photo by Miles Gregory, © 2019.

P.198 – Photo by Timothy Jules Hull | www.globaltimoto.com, © 2017.

P.99 – Photo by Miles Gregory, © 2019.

P.115 – TOP: Photo by Miles Gregory, © 2019. BOTTOM: Sir Oliver Mar-text vomits into the audience during As You Like It (Dir. Tom Mallaburn), Auckland 2017. Photo by Peter Meecham, © Pop-up Globe International Ltd 2017. Used under fair dealing for educational commentary and critical analysis.

P.116 – TOP: Henry V cuts the Constable of France's throat, blood sprays into the audience, in Henry V (Dir. Miles Gregory), Auckland 2017. Photo by Peter Meecham, © Pop-up Globe International Ltd 2017. Used under fair dealing for educational commentary and critical analysis. BOTTOM: Photo by Miles Gregory, © 2017.

P.117 – TOP: Photo by Miles Gregory, © 2017. BOTTOM: Photo by Miles Gregory © 2017.

P.118 - Photo by Miles Gregory, © 2017.

P.119 – Photo by Benny Vandergast, Wikimedia Commons, CC BY-SA 4.0.

P.120 – Photo by Benny Vandergast, Wikimedia Commons, CC BY-SA 4.0. BOTTOM: Photo by Miles Gregory, © 2019.

P.140 – TOP: Touchstone shows 'rock-star' energy during As You Like It (Dir. Tom Mallaburn), Auckland 2017. Photo by Peter Meecham, © Pop-up Globe International Ltd 2017. Used under fair dealing for educational commentary and critical analysis. BOTTOM: Dr Pinch leads the disguised comic ensemble in The Comedy of Errors (Dir. Miles Gregory). Photo by Peter Meecham, © Pop-up Globe International Ltd 2018. Used under fair dealing for educational commentary and critical analysis.

P.141– TOP: Photo by Benny Vandergast, Wikimedia Commons, CC BY-SA 4.0. BOTTOM: Photo by Benny Vandergast, Wikimedia Commons, CC BY-SA 4.0.

P.142 – TOP & BOTTOM: Photo by Miles Gregory, © 2018.

P.143 – TOP: Photo by Miles Gregory, © 2017. BOTTOM: Photo by Benny Vandergast, Wikimedia Commons, CC BY-SA 4.0.

About the author

DR. MILES GREGORY IS a theatre director, scholar, and cultural entrepreneur whose groundbreaking work has transformed how audiences experience Shakespeare today. He is the founder and former Artistic Director of Pop-up Globe (2015–2020), the world's first full-scale touring reconstruction of Shakespeare's second Globe Theatre. Under his leadership, Pop-up Globe became the largest theatre company in the Southern Hemisphere, performing to 750,000 audience members across Australasia and winning fifteen major theatre awards.

He was educated at King's College, Auckland, before reading for a BA in Modern History at Durham University, an MFA in Staging Shakespeare at Exeter University, and a PhD in Shakespeare in Performance at Bristol University.

Dr. Gregory has directed over fifty professional Shakespeare productions worldwide. At 23, he became the youngest director in London's West End, staging *Hamlet* and *Twelfth Night* at the Westminster Theatre. He has founded, led and advised state funded theatres and independent Shakespeare festivals around the world, and served as a visiting lecturer at London's Royal Central School of Speech & Drama. In 2018 he was recognized for his leadership in New Zealand's arts and culture sector with the prestigious Blake Leader Award.

Beyond theatre, Dr. Gregory has pioneered immersive storytelling and digital innovation, co-founding HyperCinema, an AI-driven interactive storytelling platform, in 2023. He is married to historical costume specialist Bob Capocci, formerly Head of Costume Design at Pop-up Globe. Together they have created dozens of productions over the last twenty-five years.

www.ingramcontent.com/pod-product-compliance
Lightning Source LLC
Chambersburg PA
CBHW041957090426
42811CB00014B/1525